My Child Sees
MONSTERS

Simple Steps to Send Them Away

ANN MARIE MORA
LYNN DONOVAN

THREE KEYS PUBLISHING
Books to Live By

THREE KEYS PUBLISHING
Books to Live By

Published by Three Keys Ministries
Temecula, California, U.S.A.
www.threekeysministries.com
Printed in the U.S.A.
© 2021 Ann Marie Mora & Lynn Donovan
All rights reserved.
Print: 978-0-9986000-8-6

Book cover and interior design by Dineen Miller: Designer Girl Graphics, www.dineenmiller.com

CONTENTS

ENDORSEMENTS

"Finally, a biblical resource to help parents navigate the very real spiritual issues our children face. Disney has been the most influential voice in dealing with monsters for far too long! Annie and Lynn combine storytelling with biblical education and give parents practical tools to deal with these difficult issues. It's a must have for parents with spiritually gifted children."
—**Sue Robson,** Owner, Life Coach, and Spiritual Director, LifeSource Coaches

"What a learning experience reading Lynn and Ann Marie's book. I felt Ann Marie's frustration in crying out for assistance to help her supernaturally gifted children. This cry went unmet by doctors, as well as the clergy. Thankfully, as she gained knowledge into the spiritual realm, she and her husband were able to lead their children. Lynn Donovan's vast knowledge of the spiritual realm, spiritual gifts, and our authority in Christ, coupled with Ann Marie's knowledge and experience, makes this book a must read for parents whose children are gifted in the supernatural. I might also add that this book is also a learning tool for anyone wanting to gain knowledge in these areas — I was mesmerized."
—**Martha Bush**, Author of *Helping Hurting Children: A Journey of Healing, Winning Them With Prayer,* and writer at LynnDonovan.com

"As parents of spiritually gifted children, we found this book to be incredibly encouraging and life-giving. This book inspired our personal walk with God and gave us practical tools and hope as we guide our children in their God-given gifts."
—**Justin and Chelsea Kenton,** Lead Pastors of Living Stones Church

"Reading *My Child Sees Monsters* was one of the best investments that I've made for my children. This book is filled with simple tools to help any parent who is seeking to understand the spiritual realm. I have a better understanding about spiritual gifts and senses which helps me to understand the gifts my children have. I also know the importance of stewarding these gifts in my children. I am learning about the authority that I've been given through the blood of Jesus to command and cleanse my home. This is a powerful weapon to combat the night terrors or demonic influences that have been tormenting my children. With this book, through the guidance of the Holy Spirit, I can teach my children how to stand in their authority and help them strengthen and use their gifts. Both Lynn and Ann Marie have a wonderful way with words. I have been blessed by their experiences and knowledge. Their work will truly bless my family for generations to come."

—**Tiffany Carter,** Writer

"This is such an important book! The Bible tells us that our enemies are not of flesh and blood but evil spiritual beings that attack us from "an unseen realm." (Ephesians 6:12 NLT) These "monsters" are cowardly and delight in striking terror into our precious children. *My Child Sees Monsters* wisely advises that when our spiritually sensitive children catch true glimpses of these frightening demons, we need to believe them and fight alongside them. This book encouraged me to nurture and guide my children in their God-given gifts, and gave me the tools to cleanse and protect our home and to teach my children the truth of the power of their position as a Child of God. This book actually teaches them spiritual self-defense from a young age! With these skills they can be free from fear and ultimately be empowered to slay their own monsters! No more sleepless nights!"

—**Lori Wangler,** Teacher, Songwriter/Voice Coach, Mother of five

"As a mother of a spiritually gifted child, I highly recommend reading this book! *My Child Sees Monsters* has provided myself and my son confirmation as well as answers that have encouraged us in our spiritual journey together. Thank you, Annie and Lynn!"

—Monica Harper

"This book helped me understand my own childhood. My sister and I shared a bedroom when we were kids and now as adults, we've come to realized that we both endured extreme fear every night. She saw a figure and I always sensed it. We would lay there paralyzed as a demon of fear stood in our door watching us. This book provides the tools that will help anyone discover their God-given gifts. You will also learn how to protect your home from demons and become aware of the spiritual realm that surrounds us. I am beyond blessed to have had the opportunity to read this book and to come away with tools to defend myself against the things that lurk in the night. I can feel the presence of the Lord in this book and will be recommending this book to everyone I know."

—Katie Marsh, Seer

"*My Child Sees Monsters* is a unique guide for parents, grandparents, and anyone who interacts with young children. It addresses the spiritual realm in straightforward fashion with Biblically-sound principles and first-hand experience. I can say without exaggerating that had I understood the contents of this book when my own children were small, my life and theirs could have been drastically different."

—Jeanne Ritari

"This book is a must have for any/all parents to read. Whether your child is one who 'sees' into the supernatural or not, all of our children have spiritual giftings waiting to be nurtured. This book outlines practical steps to seeing those. I wish I had this book when my children were young. I would have been able to assist my children because I would have known what to do. My son wouldn't have had to suffer with night terrors for years! Well written, practical and applicable advice and strategies in kingdom living! A must have for every parent's library."

—**LuAnn Wendover**

"I have had the joy and blessing of working alongside Annie Mora for over three years as a leader in children's ministry and as an educator. She is a deeply gifted and empathetic advocate for children, parents, and families. Her giftings are numerous, but most powerfully among them is her capacity to hear from Heaven and to equip kids to do the same. Her writing will encourage you and your children, give powerful permission for your child's supernatural experiences, and invite you into a fuller prophetic family life. She writes from experience and deep intimacy with Holy Spirit. It is my privilege to support her work to see children empowered in their spiritual gifts!"

—**Tracy Brown**, CPSOM Dean of Academics

*To every parent and child who
courageously embraces the supernatural
Kingdom of the Living God!*

The Mora Family

Thank you, Father, Jesus, and Holy Spirit.

*Jesus said, "Let the little children come to me,
and do not hinder them, for the kingdom of heaven belongs to such as these."*
MATTHEW 19:14

ACKNOWLEDGMENTS

Ann Marie would like to thank:

My husband and family for encouraging me to share our experiences publicly. I also would like to thank Lynn Donovan for believing me as I revealed our story. Also, for equipping myself and my family spiritually and providing encouragement in ways she will never fully realize. Thank you, Lynn, for coaching and standing by me, and for the prompting and timing of this book. It will be a gem for those out there like me.

Lynn would like to thank:

Annie Mora for her courage and faith to publicly share her story and her passion to encourage parents who are facing what she has lived. Well done!

Thank you Dineen Miller. Your design work continues to reflect the creativity of a Master, our Father. Thank you for sharing your gifts and crafting a beautiful cover and book interior.

Editor: Denise Harmer. Thank you for editing yet another work from my heart. You continue to partner with me to create an offering of excellence unto the Lord.

INTRODUCTION

He called a little child to him, and placed the child among them. And he said: "Truly I tell you, unless you change and become like little children, you will never enter the kingdom of heaven. Therefore, whoever takes the lowly position of this child is the greatest in the kingdom of heaven. And whoever welcomes one such child in my name welcomes me."
MATTHEW 18:2-5

Mom and dad, we, the authors, acknowledge the noble undertaking that is before you. You are the chosen parents who will steward the future prophets, seers, and leaders of the Kingdom of God. We understand the enormity you face as you guide, protect, and nurture the life of your spiritually sensitive child. Your role is vitally important! This directive is also tremendously challenging.

As parents ourselves, we are passionately motivated to educate and equip you with the truth regarding spiritually gifted children, and to help you to step out of anxiety and confusion which plagues many families. We offer real-life experiences, lessons, and practical suggestions to guide you into understanding about the spirit world that your children sense and see.

Through the pages, expect an overview of various spiritual gifts that are commonplace within our children. Together we will uncover how our kids acquired these unusual gifts. We'll explore the reality that a number of our children will displace their gifting as they mature. And we'll discover why some retain their supernatural awareness into adulthood.

We will also explore the effective course of action to assist your children to step out of fear and into safety as they learn to engage their gifts through courage and love. We will point you to the source of all spiritual gifting. We'll consider the parenting errors that occur in the process when searching desperately for peace and insight. We offer you a turning place as well as hope. It is possible for your home to be a place of peace and comfort for the entire family.

Contained within these pages is our humble contribution of experience and gained wisdom. We recognize this book isn't an exhaustive study of all that is available to guide you and your children through their spiritual giftings. However, it's filled with a significant number of practical tips and suggestions to change the dynamic of your home and parenting. It is a place to begin.

You can help your children step into their spiritual identity, thereby contributing to their future success.

MEET ANN MARIE

For the Spirit God gave us does not make us timid, but gives us power, love and self-discipline.
2 TIMOTHY 1:7

Hi, mom and dad. I'm Ann Marie, please call me Annie. I grew up in southern California on a horse ranch along with every kind of farm animal. At a young age, I intuitively understood that there was more to this world than merely the visible. When I was eleven, I asked Jesus into my heart. However, it wasn't until I was twenty-seven that I began to comprehend the depths of this relationship.

I was raised without faith guidance, but I'm convinced my curiosity about God and even my own spiritual gifts are a legacy from my grandparents, who were pastors. When I grew into adulthood, like many, I discovered life was incredibly difficult and uncertain. When my children were small, a day arrived when I cried out to God from a place of absolute desperation, "God, is this it? Is this my life and then I die?"

At that moment a friend of mine burst into my house shouting, "You have got to read *The Purpose Driven Life*. It is so good!" When she left my house, I investigated, then purchased the book. I remember thinking how weird it was that within a split second, God answered my prayer. Turns out, this book provided the direction I needed. Upon reading it, I rededicated my life to Christ.

As of the writing of this book, I have been married for twenty-two years to my husband, Josh. God has blessed us with three beautiful children—Joshua, Ben, and Carly. I'll share more about them later. I love spending time in the Lord's presence while gardening, watching my wacky chickens, walking the dog, or hiking with the family. I have a blast singing worship songs in the car while my kids beg me to stop because my voice is only, ahem—unto the Lord!

My heart for children is huge. I love teaching kids at church. My professional background is special needs children's paraeducator. Additionally, I nurtured small humans through my home daycare for more than 16 years. I'm committed to helping young people as they learn and develop their God-given gifts.

I've navigated through uncharted territory over the last 21 years, parenting my three extraordinary and spiritually gifted children. I'm convinced the Christian church rarely speaks about what we have lived. I realize that supernaturally sensitive children are nearly always rejected because the church is afraid to believe their experiences are real. Additionally, as parents we are unaware, uneducated, and fearful. Because of our fear we're inclined to help our children turn off their gifts without contemplating their importance and that their gifting is necessary for their highest achievements.

It was my faith in God that sustained and pushed me forward in the lonely years. However, with the Lord's guidance and wisdom, coupled with the gifting of a mother's love, I slowly became aware that my kids had something out of this world.

I could see the treasure in their eyes! The gifts my kids were born with are like a beautiful treasure chest, adorned with the most valuable gemstones covering the outside and even more extravagant wonder waiting to be unlocked on the inside.

As a young mom, I longed for a book such as this when I was

traveling the dusty road of confusion, feeling lost and alone. That is why I'm committed to sharing my story, wisdom, and experiences with you.

Thank you for allowing me to be a voice of love and trust to assure you that your children's giftings are a good thing, and with a little guidance, the anxiety will fade away. You and your child will make it through feeling happier, confident, rested, and relaxed. I offer a number of powerful tools and takeaways that are practical and helpful.

When other's opinions of your family's unique experiences create confusion or pain, we will face the challenges together. As you are likely aware, there are days that are incredibly difficult but eventually you will find people who believe you, just as I did. And you will discover there are those who also offer sound biblical evidence that spiritual gifts are real and that people operate in them all the time.

I pray that as you read through the pages you will experience peace, discover joy in your child's uniqueness, and also find a love and excitement to develop the gifts inside your kids. And then, perhaps, unlock the gifts that reside within yourself.

I bless you with this powerful passage from the Word of God.

For God's gifts and his call are irrevocable.
ROMANS 11:29

MEET LYNN

Take delight in the Lord, and he will give you the desires of your heart.
PSALM 37:4

From one parent to another, this parenting thing is tough! Tiny lives are under our care and instruction, but for a moment. Childhood passes quickly.

As of the writing of this book, I've been parenting for nearly 40 years. My children are grown and have children of their own. I made many mistakes along the way, and yet, sometimes I found myself nurturing my children forward with bright success, but by the grace of God. Throughout my parenting years, my faith in Jesus Christ is what I leaned upon. I also looked to the Word of God for help and assurances.

I've partnered with Annie to help parents in the trenches to comprehend some of the most unique aspects of raising a child who is sensitive to the spiritual world.

Annie's experiences with her gifted children offers specific examples and stories. I bring my considerable knowledge about the spiritual realm and the supernatural gifts of God. And I bring my writing and publishing background.

I've teamed up with Annie to impart truth about what she and many parents face when raising a spiritually sensitive child. I am motivated by compassion and the reality that supernatural gifts are from God and are beautiful.

Regretfully, too often supernatural gifts are misunderstood and are viewed as terrifying and unwanted. Parents who are desperate for answers turn toward the occult, new age ideas, or psychics to help explain away what is occurring in their home. I'm grieved that the Christian church has remained silent for decades regarding spiritually gifted children. The church has abandoned these parents and kids, labeled them, and shoved them out the door.

It's time that believers in Jesus step up to help parents and children learn about their gifts. It's now that we must teach mom and dad and a generation of little ones how to walk with confidence and purpose in what God has bestowed upon them.

I'm a pastor and have been in public ministry for more than 15 years. I'm the Executive Director of Three Keys Ministries, a healing/deliverance prayer ministry, publishing house, and spiritual growth training center. I'm an award-winning author, speaker, and spiritual formation coach.

The many years of public ministry experience lends itself to solid Biblical teaching and practical knowledge. I've written a number of books that remain widely read, including a parenting book. I am a sold-out believer in Jesus Christ. It's my honor to pray with people worldwide to bring them into greater healing, wholeness, and deliverance from the oppression of the devil through my prayer, healing, and spiritual formation ministries. I have a storehouse of knowledge and experience regarding the Kingdom of God and the spiritual realm. I walk with authority and power of the Holy Spirit. It's my desire to pass all that I know along to the next generation.

My passion is to lead believers into intimacy with God the Father, Jesus Christ, and the Holy Spirit and into our full identity as a child of the Most High God. I live in Temecula, California with my husband, Mike and our two wacky dogs. Finn and Gracie.

Annie and I are privileged to walk this journey with you. Thank you for your trust.

Jesus, I bring before you this mom or dad who is searching for answers for their child. I ask that you cover them with your blood and protect them with warrior angels. Dispatch angelic sentries to stand at the doors of their home and place a ring of holy fire around them and their children for protection from evil.

Lord, bless them to step out of fear and into the wisdom of heaven. Lead them as they lead their children. Teach this mom/dad everything he or she must know to become an exceptional parent who will shepherd their young-sters into their purpose which was written before time began. Bless them with the peace of heaven. Walk with them every day. In your name, Jesus, I pray. AMEN

Your eyes saw my unformed body; all the days ordained for me were written in your book before one of them came to be.
PSALM 139:16

I SEE ANGELS

Ann Marie

Are not all angels ministering spirits sent to serve those who will inherit salvation?
HEBREWS 1:14

"Mommy, did you know there are angels flying in a circle over our house?"

Just moments earlier I peered through the kitchen curtains. A smile tipped my lips as I watched through the glass as my kids played together in the warmth of a southern California summer.

This memory remains crystal clear as it was precisely at this moment when my life altered forever. My two-year-old daughter ran into the kitchen and up to me as I arranged lunch plates on the table. She wrapped her arms about my leg. I remember looking down into the impetuous excitement reflected in her baby browns.

"Mommy, did you know there are angels flying in a circle over our house?"

I stared at this child as she quizzed up at me.

What do you do with a statement like this? Recalling this moment today, my eyes well up as I consider my response and how my words or attitude might have affected her little heart.

I was silent. I brushed her off with my quiet confusion, wran-

1

gling over what she just spoke. In those early years with three small kids and my in-home daycare business, I was frantically busy. And like most parents, I'd learned to parent from my parents, peers, and professionals such as our pediatricians and school counselors. I was assured over and again, until I was nearly convinced, that children who see angels are merely engaged in wild imagination.

Considering my daughter's words, I thought to myself, *this adorable child really is cute with her fantastic imagination. But I really need to finish placing lunch on the table and round up the rest to wash up and eat.*

I hope I smiled an acknowledgement her way. I don't remember. But I hope I did.

Childhood chatter continued around the lunch table as I sat processing my daughter's words. This sweet little girl wandered into the kitchen and spoke something extraordinary. Did I believe her? Are angels real?

WHAT???

I wonder how many of you have lived a similar experience with your children. What are you supposed to do when your child, of an innocent age, pronounces that angels are flying overhead? I'll tell you this, your thoughts oblige the contemplation of a number of random questions.

Is she really seeing something?

She is so young. How could she be making this up?

Is it a spiritual thing or did she see a cloud in the sky?

Is this child of sound mind?

Is her imagination running away with her?

These questions implore further questions.

Are angels even real?

WTH! (Can I say that in a Christian book? But that's how I felt at the time. I'm sure many of you relate.)

I felt alone as the questions flooded my soul. I was walking a road without anyone to guide me. Which brings me to the first powerful tool that every parent must be equipped with.

You are not alone.

You aren't the only parent who has a child engaged in the spiritual realm. In fact, a good number of parents are in the middle of your experience as well. However, most also believe their child's spiritual experience is unique and no one else in the entire world is going through what you are facing.

It's simply not true.

I've inquired of parents and discovered a good number will admit that one or all of their children have engaged in angel encounters, glimpsed frightening beings, or saw or sensed things that aren't visible. Like me, they also concluded their child was too young to be making it up. Or their child's visceral reactions to what they were experiencing went far beyond normal childhood imagination or fear.

I'm convinced that the greatest gift Lynn and I will impart to you is the relief that arrives when you realize you aren't alone and that you and your kid are not crazy. And the second gift is this—there is hope and there are satisfactory answers.

So, today, take a deep breath and exhale a giant sigh of relief. We are in this together and we will quickly walk you through several common issues and offer you simple steps to navigate your future and develop a healthy spirituality for yourself and your child.

The best way to navigate forward is to establish a firm foundation on which to construct our road to peace. We must start with the truth.

TRUTH

Lynn

Then you will know the truth, and the truth will set you free.
JOHN 8:32

Our purpose as authors is to displace misconceptions about spiritual experiences and gain a view that offers truth, hope, and peace. The highest and best source for practical and reliable truth about the spiritual is the Bible.

The Word of God is a book about God, who is a spirit and his Kingdom is the spiritual realm. Through the Bible we are offered an invitation into understanding. I realize there are a number of people who are looking for answers but aren't familiar with the Bible, God, or the spirit realm. My heart is filled with compassion and assurances for every desperate parent who is on the search for help.

Because the church hasn't offered an alternative explanation or direction to parents until recently, far too many moms and dads have turned to alternatives born of occult sources to explain the phenomenon occurring in their homes. These sources, however, produce a compromised and even dangerous view of the spiritual world. Ultimately, if followed for too long, it will lead unsuspecting people into darkness and finally a lost eternity. These realms are ruled by demonic powers that offer a perverted reality and a distorted perception of the spiritual.

Many people naturally turn to the Christian church for answers but regrettably are met with ignorance, fear, and rejection. As a pastor, I offer my sincere apologies to anyone who looked to the Church and received condemnation instead of acceptance and help. Please forgive us, the church pastors, and clergy, who failed you.

But NO LONGER! The spiritual realm belongs to us, the believers in Christ. Our Father in heaven, the angelic and much more dwell in the realm of the spiritual and in heaven. We are all invited into that realm through the Word of God.

Take a look at this invitation:

So let us come boldly to the throne of our gracious God. There we will receive his mercy, and we will find grace to help us when we need it most.
HEBREWS 4:16

This passage offers us an audience with God. We may approach boldly and ask for his assistance in our time of need. This applies to those of us who are raising children. We need God's wisdom, help, and explanations. We need his goodness and instruction as we wade through the various experiences we encounter in our home, with our kids, and in this world.

The Bible is our go-to source for truth. When we view our experiences through this lens, we will find honesty and explanations that continually points us toward love, peace, joy, and goodness.

*For the **kingdom of God** is not a matter of eating and drinking but of **righteousness and peace and joy** in the Holy Spirit.*
ROMANS 14:17

Do you remember the questions at the beginning of the chapter? We will unpack these along with others and allow God to

5

impart wisdom and heavenly perspective on our inquiries. The Word of God offers a sound and unchanging platform on which to stand and truth that benefits humanity century upon century.

If you aren't quite there about faith, Christ, and all that, don't put this book down yet. Because Annie and I promise we have real answers and hope for you regardless of where you are in your discovery of faith. Read along and discover that it's simple to understand the Kingdom of God. And God's solutions are uncomplicated. They are real, effective, and filled with love.

One more thing. Every single person on this planet is invited into the Kingdom of our Father through Jesus, his son. If at any point while reading this book God draws you into his love and you desire to live within his Kingdom for the rest of your days and all eternity, you are absolutely welcomed. In the appendix you will find simple steps for salvation followed by a prayer you can pray to receive salvation and an eternal family through the Son of God. Turn there any time and pray aloud and step into the Kingdom of God.

With our source defined, we will move forward and tackle the topics such as night terrors, dark angels, open doors, etc.

In the same way, there is joy in the presence of God's angels when even one sinner repents.
LUKE 15:10

ARE ANGELS REAL

Lynn

See that you do not despise one of these little ones. For I tell you that their
angels in heaven always see the face of my Father in heaven.
MATTHEW 18:10

Let's tackle a few of those questions from the beginning of this
chapter.

Are angels real?

Is my kid seeing something real or imagining something?

How do I navigate through this?

One of my favorite stories about angels is found in Matthew 18.
I referenced it above. This verse affirms that every child has an
angel. There are sections throughout the Bible that speak of
angels. Angels brought the good news of the birth of the Savior to
the shepherds. Angels appear from cover to cover and are a vital
part of God's Kingdom and interact with humanity regularly.

We are assured angels are real beings sent from God, and we
learn that angels have various purposes and functions. What most
people struggle with is this—do angels interact with people today?
The short answer, yes. AND they are more active than you think
or believe.

As a side note, one day in eternity you will meet your assigned angel and come to learn that this angel saved you from certain death or disaster a number of times throughout your life.

Are not all angels ministering spirits sent to serve those who will inherit salvation?
HEBREWS 1:14

Let's contend with the next obvious question. Why does my child see angels?

2

THE SPIRITUAL REALM

Lynn

Start children off on the way they should go, and even when they are old
they will not turn from it.
PROVERBS 22:6

R aising children is extraordinary!
Within their innocence we perceive the truest notions about ourselves. We were made for love. We were created to experience joy, laughter, to dance in wonderment within creation that surrounds us. Our design is royalty and we have been invited into a family. Our purpose on earth is to learn to love and receive love from our heavenly Father.

We are children ourselves at the core, a reality most of us abandoned years ago. We are three-part beings. We are a spirit, with a soul, and we live within a human body. The truth is humans were designed to continually be aware of our heavenly, supernatural home and to intimately know and live within the love and persistent communication with God.

Our family is extensive through our common belief in the Savior of the world, Jesus Christ. We were created for a purpose. And our objectives for this earth are supported and nurtured through the many gifts that come from God. As humans, spiritual gifts are part of our original design. When we learn to use our gifts to love people and to partner our gifts in agreement with heaven, we thrive. We enjoy a life of satisfaction, dignity, and triumph. We fulfill the scripture mandate, on earth as it is in heaven.

Your kingdom come, your will be done, on earth as it is in heaven.
MATTHEW 6:10

SPIRITUAL BIRTH

Lynn

Your eyes saw my unformed body; all the days ordained for me were written in your book before one of them came to be.
PSALM 139:16

Little kids are fascinating. My encounters with pre-verbal children are delightful and filled with wonder. Allow me to share an example.

Recently I was walking among the vineyards near my home on my morning walk-n-pray, when a young couple and their toddler son were outside speaking with neighbors. The little boy, of course, was the center of entertainment as he waved and teetered about while the adults visited.

But something fascinating occurred, which tends to be a consistent experience when I'm around small children whom I've never met. I stepped up close to the group to scoot around them, but as I did, the little boy paused in his tracks and looked straight at me. A brilliant smile formed on his face that lit the morning. His gaze moved to just above my right shoulder. He smiled, then giggled.

I smiled back knowingly. This little man was catching a glimpse of the angels that are always behind me. This small child was remembering or experiencing the spiritual realm. He was revisiting a memory/awareness/gift of the Lord, the angelic, and the spiritual realm.

I waved at him. He smiled broadly. His parents were now mesmerized by his giggling, yet utterly unaware of what their tiny child was experiencing.

I grinned to myself because I knew exactly what the little guy was looking at. I knew his heart was blessed to perceive the angels. I was blessed and the Lord was blessed because this small child was connecting to his true home. I'm not able to fully explain why young, pre-verbal children are highly aware of the spiritual realm, but I find this is common.

I wonder if you've experienced something similar with your child. Young children appear to easily perceive the spiritual world that surrounds us. The angelic, demonic, and much more exists and are intertwined within our physical world. This realm is continually in motion, good and evil.

Over the years I've become keenly aware that many of us perceived the spiritual as toddlers. However, for the most part, we shut down our ability about the time we began to take on language. This occurs roughly around age two.

But not for all.

There are those who retain their spiritual perceptions for a lifetime. And that is the intent and purpose of heaven, that all of humanity would be endowed with spiritual gifts for life. We are God's kids. It's our birthright to function in the giftings of our Father. Our purpose is to learn to appropriately shoulder our gifts and use them in concert with the will of God. It's also our privilege to perceive and interact with our heavenly home, the spiritual realm, and release heaven into the earth.

I remember a story Annie told me about her eldest son, Josh, who at the time was a one-year-old. She was tickling him after a fresh diaper change. While they were giggling, he stopped suddenly, became wide-eyed as he looked up at the vaulted ceiling.

He pointed his small finger upward. To Annie's astonishment he whispered in amazement, "Papa!"

Her son's giggles drew the face of Father God, who came to look upon the joy of his child. The baby also caught a glimpse of his heavenly Father. I remember that Annie pondered this encounter, questioning, "Who is Papa? Is there really something more than what I see in this world? I wish I could see what he sees. Is this even biblical?"

I know there are scripture verses that affirm we are known by the Lord even in the womb.

Before I formed you in the womb I knew you, before you were born I set you apart; I appointed you as a prophet to the nations.
JEREMIAH 1:5

Your eyes saw my unformed body; all the days ordained for me were written in your book before one of them came to be.
PSALM 139:16

For those God foreknew he also predestined to be conformed to the image of his Son, that he might be the firstborn among many brothers and sisters.
ROMANS 8:29

But when God, who set me apart from my mother's womb and called me by his grace, was pleased.
GALATIANS 1:15

Gaining an understanding of how gifts are imparted, received, and stewarded into adulthood brings us peace. Peace that we are able to impart to our kids, no matter their age or gifting.

BELIEVE

Ann Marie

The angel said to him, "I am Gabriel. I stand in the presence of God, and I have been sent to speak to you and to tell you this good news.
LUKE 1:19

A short number of days following the "angels flying over the house" event, I was tidying the kitchen when Carly bounced in and popped up on the barstool, chattering away, matter-of-factly. She said, "Mommy, there is an angel outside on the swing. He told me his name is Gabriel. He wants to talk to you."

I froze for a second, once more, shocked.

Oh, this child!

I quickly glanced out the window at the wooden swing that hung from our patio cover, yearning to catch a glimpse of this Gabriel. The timing of Carly's proclamation was significant. I'd been reading the book of Daniel in the Bible. I wondered how on earth could she possibly know this story. No one had told her about Gabriel. NO ONE!

Once again I remained silenced by her announcement as I processed this new angel revelation. "How on earth did she know the name of the angel I'd just read about in the Bible?" I knew from my study that this angel, Gabriel, is the one who brings insight and understanding in response to Daniel's vision and his prayer.

Gabriel is also the messenger who appeared to Zechariah, the High Priest. He informed the somewhat stunned man that his wife was pregnant. Gabriel supplied the name of Zechariah's unborn son, John.

As I contemplated what I'd learned about Gabriel, I continued to peek through the window hoping to catch a glimpse of him standing on the front porch, but to no avail. I secretly tucked away this experience intending to process the implications later.

Still, today, when I remember this exchange with my daughter, I can't help but wonder, *What was my daughter thinking or perceiving through my non-committal response?* I regret that I missed an opportunity to talk with her about what she saw and I also missed an extraordinary encounter with an angel.

At the time, I simply wasn't prepared to believe, as I was only beginning to learn myself.

I was learning through her.

TWO MORE POSITIVE SIMPLE FIRST STEPS

Ann Marie

Then Jesus told him, "Because you have seen me, you have believed; blessed are those who have not seen and yet have believed.
JOHN 20:29

In my reflections upon the years of my children's encounters with the spiritual realm, I have gained substantial wisdom. And considering what I've shared about angels, allow me to provide a truth that will release you into greater peace and give your child hope.

Choose to believe.

Believe it's real. Choose to believe your child. Your affirmation of their reality will dissipate their fear.

Somewhere deep within me, in spite of my lack of spiritual knowledge, I earnestly began to believe and embrace the truth that my kids were interacting with the spiritual realm. I decided one day to simply believe them. I chose to believe they weren't crazy. They were seeing something I couldn't perceive. But I chose to believe them and believe the spirit realm was real.

I appreciate this is a giant leap for any parent. The world around us preaches respectable reasons, other than spiritual, as to why our kids see things we can't. They range from the silly to the frightening.

But these are the beginning steps to peace. So, allow me to share the first two simple and powerful steps:

- Know you aren't alone.
- Choose to believe your child and believe there is a spiritual realm where angels, Father God, Jesus, and goodness reigns.

3

NIGHT TERRORS AND THINGS THAT GO BUMP IN THE NIGHT

Ann Marie

For God is not a God of disorder but of peace.
1 CORINTHIANS 14:33a

Our small family celebrated Carly's fifth birthday. Three years passed since the Gabriel visit when one afternoon she said, "Mommy, did you know there are good angels and there are bad angels? The good angels are really bright with lots of cool colors. The bad ones are ugly and dark."

This time I didn't freeze. Since the Gabriel incident, I was anticipating and hoping for another spiritual experience where I was prepared to ask a question in response. "Carly, do you see bad angels too?"

"Yes, and they come in through a dark hole in the ground."

I'll remind you, she was five years old!

She proceeded to draw me a picture. I stared in astonishment as she revealed the good angels who were brightly colored and in flight in the sky near the sun. The dark angels were underground (under the grass) with a black hole next to them. Carly pointed to the black hole and said emphatically, "Mommy, that's how they get

ANN MARIE MORA & LYNN DONOVAN

in. And this orange one," she pointed with her tiny finger, "is a very bad man. He tells the dark angels what to do."

Angels Flying

Bad man who tells demons what to do

Demons below
Coming out of pit

Carly, Age Five

Once again, this small, adorable, and compelling child sent my "safe-life" careening over the edge, into a new reality. Numerous questions sprang to mind in rapid succession, demanding some semblance of acceptable answers to satisfy and restore my reliable and ordinary world. How could a five-year-old know about Satan, demons, and how could she possibly know that demons arise out of a pit? The probable answers to these questions were stunning, frightening, and impossible.

My initial reaction was concern. *Was my daughter scared?* Which led me to, *should I be scared? Why are there bad angels?* My mind demanded answers. *And where do they come from?* I shook my head, pondering, *Is this real?*

On and on my thoughts whirled, spinning out more questions than solutions, and confusion became my companion. Finally, the most paralyzing thoughts arose. *What will my husband think? After all, he's a new Christian. I can't tell him. He'll think we are both nuts. Oh my, I can't tell anybody, they will all think Carly is nuts! Is anybody safe? Is anybody else experiencing this?*

It's a scary place to face the possibility that your kid sees angels and demons and you have no idea what you are supposed to do about it. Coupled with the need to protect and also to understand what is actually occurring, the battles will rage within your mind and extend to cover a vast territory of frightening answers. The fight is a battle within yourself, determining what you believe. You earnestly search the depths of your mind and worldview to resolve the question: Is my child legitimate or perhaps requires a visit to a psych ward? You discover you are contending for yourself and your child's mental and emotional health.

In my journey, there wasn't a single person I felt was safe to lean upon. I remember at the time asking my pastors for advice. Their "well-meaning" recommendation was to take my kids to a pediatrician. That office visit left me with additional confusion and fear. As professionals, they were directing me to medicate my children. But I knew in my heart what was true about my kids. They were not mentally ill. They were seeing in the spiritual realm.

I knew instinctively with a deep conviction that medicating Carly wasn't the answer. She was a sweet and ordinary girl. I wasn't going to medicate her into oblivion. And please listen to me, there are situations and children who need medication to help them. I believe in the medical field. But I had a tiny bit of faith within and I knew that I knew that I knew, in my knower, that medication wasn't the answer for my children. I became convinced she would continue to see these spiritual manifestations, medicated or not, as she'd been seeing them since she was born.

It was my faith in God that sustained me. His guidance, wisdom, and the gifting of a mother's love that led to a peaceful conviction that my kids had something out of this world. I could see the treasure in their eyes!

Shortly after the office visit our family sank into a dark spiral that felt extremely out of control and appeared to have no end in sight. It was lonely.

THE STRUGGLE IN THE DEMONIC REALM

Ann Marie

*For our struggle is not against flesh and blood, but against the rulers, against
the authorities, against the powers of this dark world and against the
spiritual forces of evil in the heavenly realms.*
EPHESIANS 6:12

All hell broke loose.

On occasion, Carly would wake up in the night crying, absolutely terrified. In the beginning my husband and I managed to
comfort her back to sleep in her own bed. However, as time
passed, the frequency of her night terrors increased and she
refused to stay in her own room when awakened from the fear. Her
sleep disruptions reached the point where she absolutely refused
to go into her room alone after dark. Finally, she stopped going
into her room to play during the day. Carly began to avoid her
bedroom completely. Her room was a part of our home, but
completely abandoned and unused.

At some point she began climbing into our bed routinely
following her nightly bath. She felt safe with us and reluctantly we
adjusted because the three of us were desperate for sleep.

However, one night I decided the sleeping arrangement must
change for the stability of my marriage. It was time Carly learned

to sleep in her own bed! The night arrived that I determined Carly would sleep in her room. I began preparing her by stating a warning. "Tonight after your shower you will go to bed in your own bed."

"NO!" she screamed, turning white as a ghost.

I was determined. "Yes, get used to the idea, baby girl!"

Following her shower and jammies, I picked her up and headed toward her room. She instantly tensed. The crying started immediately and by the time we reached her bedroom she was in full-out hysterics.

She grabbed the doorframe with one hand and then the other. Just as quickly as I pulled her hands off the frame, she then stuck out her foot and then grabbed hold again, scream-begging, "Don't make me go in there!"

I set her down inside the doorframe. On my knees, I looked into her eyes. "What are you afraid of?"

She pointed to her bed. "It's right there. It's on my bed. Do you see it?"

Holding back tears, I said, "No baby, I don't." Tears poured down her face and as she wiped them away, "Why don't you see it?"

I was honest. "I don't know, baby." I scooped her up into my arms and again she slept in the middle of my husband and me. I didn't know what else to do. All I knew was that I believed her and wanted to protect her.

One good thing resulted from this frightening experience. I was propelled into action.

I searched the internet, reading page after page of endless articles on the subject of child terrors. I was looking for something practical to apply. I searched for any manner of tools, prayers, anything, but came up empty. I felt utterly hopeless.

However, my searches revealed that our household wasn't the only family experiencing these night terrors. A number of articles suggested that my children were mentally ill, disturbed in some way and needed medication. However, I found nothing that was truly helpful.

Upon the heels of our nightly terrors with our youngest, next the entire family began having nightmares. One of the five of us would wake up screaming in the night. It was a bizarre season in our household.

I recall a specific night when I woke myself up screaming, then my husband shouted, and I heard my two boys down the hall scream in terror as well. In desperation we convened a family meeting the next morning.

We agreed this nighttime fright was NOT okay and we needed to find answers. One of my sons suggested that we keep our Bibles open next to our bed at night while we slept. This actually was successful for a time. We began to play praise music in the house 24/7. The music was powerfully effective, and things quieted for a long while. To this very day we continue to play praise music in our home which welcomes the good angels and the Holy Spirit.

However, the night frights continued sporadically.

One night my eldest son awoke frantic while we were dealing with another rough night terror with Carly. "Mom, I had an awful nightmare. A demon was holding me up by one leg. He had my mouth bound somehow so I couldn't yell for help. I kept struggling to yell until I finally was able to muster out, JESUS! He immediately dropped me and when he did, I fell back onto my bed. It was the fall and the thump of me hitting the bed that caused me to wake." He was white as a ghost and anxiety ridden.

This was a new low point. Weariness saturated my soul. I felt the fatigue in my bones from these extreme moments in our home.

That week I'd taken my son to a counselor. He was diagnosed schizophrenic, and of course, medication was suggested. We never went back. I knew for a fact that my kids were not schizophrenic; they were normal, happy, well-protected children that for whatever reason could "see" something I couldn't.

HOPE ARISING

Ann Marie

Come to me, all you who are weary and burdened, and I will give you rest.
MATTHEW 11:28

Night after night Carly's night terrors increased and worsened. And real night terrors are something else. Your child experiences some kind of sleep walking. I was mentally, physically, and spiritually exhausted.

I'd exhausted every avenue in search of help.

God was my last resort.

It appeared that pleading to the supreme being was all I had left. My exhaustion, however, became my awakening, a change I'd never anticipated and from which there was no turning back.

On this particular evening another draining night of terror assailed my baby daughter. Each time, her torment became tormenting for the entire family. Her terrors were brutal on us as parents because our innocent child turned into the Incredible Hulk! This never felt good and injury was inevitable no matter our efforts to keep her from breaking a limb or suffering a concussion from the flailing.

Her head would bang into my chest, then my chin. Her fingernails would dig into my skin, her grasp would pinch, her hands and feet would thrash, and her scream would pierce my very soul! I absolutely couldn't wake her and there is no reasoning. You are helpless to let it run its course. It's utterly heartbreaking.

With every ounce of energy I possessed, I'd attempt to swaddle her into safety. But that night, I reached my breaking point. I knew instinctively something was terribly wrong and I knew deep down in my gut who could fix this.

This was extraordinarily difficult for me, but the decision was made. I handed Carly to my husband, Joshua. I physically struggled to place her in his arms. I asked him to please hold her tight. And as I began to walk away from him and the screaming, he yelled down the hall, "Where are you going?" The fear of being abandoned to contain the volatility was visible on his tired face.

I didn't want to tell him that I was going to pray. I felt ashamed because I didn't know how he would respond. He told me weeks earlier he wasn't sure God was real. My faith wasn't much more than feeble. I believed that there was a God, but I lacked understanding about how to have a real relationship with him, nor did I know I needed one.

"I have to do something," was my response.

I went into my closet. I shut the door and pleaded with God. I had no idea how to pray or what to say in a situation like this. So I cried and screamed from the deepest place in my soul. I put my heart into this prayer.

"God, if you are there, will you take this from my daughter? Please take whatever evil this is. I know you can get rid of it!" Somehow, I just knew in my heart that I had to lean on him at this moment.

Instantly the screaming coming from down the hall stopped. I felt the presence of God in that closet. Upon emerging, my husband nestled our sleeping daughter in his arms.

I was blown away. Did that just happen? I prayed and then my husband and I witnessed an immediate change in Carly. I hoped my husband would be changed by this experience as well.

My dear friend, in that prayer closet I heard God say to me,

"Come to me, my dear child, with your heavy burden and I will give you rest."

This is a scripture from Matthew 11:28.

It's been eleven years since that night and my daughter remains free of night terrors. God is incredibly good and faithful. He taught me something that day. He is with me. He is with us. He is with you. He listens. He earnestly cares and is absolutely able and willing to change things.

Take my yoke upon you and learn from me, for I am gentle and humble in heart, and you will find rest for your souls.
MATTHEW 11:29

That night I returned to bed. Tears sprang to my eyes as I beheld my baby sleeping peacefully in my husband's arms. Joshua asked me, "What did you do?"

I simply informed him that I pleaded to God for help. He smiled, then rested his head against his pillow and went straight to sleep. Hmmm, was he unresponsive or just full of peace?

My friend, simple faith and a simple prayer changed everything that night. So right now, I'll share with you this next simple step.

With simple faith, pray a simple prayer like I did that night in the closet. Ask God to send away the demons and rescue your child, yourself, and your family. Then believe. Keep praying, and when things calm down give thanks for his intervention. Be persistent. Pray every night for as long as it takes. I find consistent prayers of faith will tear down years of fearful experiences and evil interference.

FEAR IS A LIAR

Ann Marie

Such love has no fear, because perfect love expels all fear. If we are afraid, it is for fear of punishment, and this shows that we have not fully experienced his perfect love.
I JOHN 4:18 NLT

M y dear friend, it becomes apparent after a number of frightening experiences that the purpose of the evil one is to scare and intimidate our innocent children. Children who have a seer gift, such as Carly, view the angelic and demonic realm. The demons typically present themselves as frightening beings to distort and create terror in our children.

Their purpose is twofold.

One, to create overwhelming fear of the spiritual, so much so, that a person chooses to reject every spiritual experience and ultimately rejects salvation through Jesus Christ.

Two, they purposely create terror to convince the individual to willingly relinquish their God-given gifts in order to stop the fear. They absolutely want the gifts shut off. Both have devastating consequences. Frequently, surrendering gifts denies the individual the fulfillment of their original design and purpose.

Let me share how the demonic engages this process.

THE BIGGEST MISTAKE

Ann Marie

For God's gifts and his call are irrevocable.
ROMANS 11:29

As my daughter grew, the night terrors ceased; however, now and again she continued to catch glimpses into the spiritual realm. Her experiences were sometimes scary as she would catch sight of shadowy, demonic beings. Because I couldn't see them, I wasn't always able to help her process what she was viewing.

When Carly was about eight years old, a significant event occurred while driving her to school one morning. We emerged from another difficult night where she wouldn't sleep because of the demonic presence that was determined to destroy her. I was so tired. I felt weary to my bones. As we drove, I began to pray in my head with a new desperation in my heart. Carly was unaware of my whispers as she sat securely buckled in the back seat.

Making our way toward her school, my question emerged. I prayed in my head, *Why, Lord? Why are you allowing my precious baby girl to go through this torment? Why are you allowing the enemy to scare the crud out of her? I'm exhausted, Lord.*

Immediately I heard his voice in response in my mind. He responded, *Hold my hand, daughter.*

At this point I simply looked over to the passenger seat and in my mind, I saw him. I instinctively reached out my right hand toward the empty seat, pretending I was holding the hand of Jesus.

Without delay Carly spoke from the back seat, "Mom, do you see Jesus? He is here with us. You're holding his hand!" Tears sprang and trailed down my cheeks as I comprehended that my daughter was viewing what I'm imagining. And I knew unequivocally within my soul that Jesus was really in the car. He was holding my hand. And I knew he was concerned and cared deeply about me and my children.

Then he said to me, *"Do you remember what you read in the book about the man who can always see in the spirit?"*

I'd read a fascinating book earlier in the year at the recommendation of our new church pastor. At the time, I'd also immersed myself in classes offered at our church which included a prophetic class, freedom classes, and a prophetic dream class. I was on a deep dive into understanding the spiritual realm. Reading this book about another person who could see in the spiritual was utterly eye-opening, and the big takeaway was that this guy could turn off his gift whenever he wanted.

With this new revelation I quickly jumped to the next logical question. *How can I teach Carly to turn off her gift when it becomes too scary?*

I'm telling you now, that was the wrong question.

So imagine, here I am sitting in the car with Jesus. He's holding my hand and speaking to me about what I'd just read in a book.

In response to Jesus and his question, I nodded my head, *Yes, Jesus, I remember.* And yes, this was what I believed Jesus was revealing to me about Carly and her gift. I could help her shut it down.

We arrived at the drop-off line at school. Coincidentally, we were early. I now sat alone with Carly. I nodded my head as a plan was forming. I knew what I needed to do.

I turned to the backseat, speaking gently to Carly. I began to explain about the man I read about in the book and that he could see good and bad angels just like her. I proceeded to explain how this man could decide in his mind to shut off his gift so he wouldn't see the spirits.

Carly cooperatively said, "I do that sometimes. I know how to do it."

"You do?" I was shocked. "Then why don't you?"

"I can?" she queried, searching for approval.

"I give you permission to shut it down when you need to. When it is too much or too scary," I reassured her.

She smiled big. Gave me a hug and kiss and then jumped out of the car. I drove off and cried all the way home. The mix of emotions about her gifts, shutting them off, combined with the reality that Jesus had been sitting in my car—it was overwhelming!

There was little to no activity after this. And my friend, this breaks my heart.

RECLAIM THE GIFT

Ann Marie

Follow the way of love and eagerly desire gifts of the Spirit, especially prophecy.

1 CORINTHIANS 14:1

My dear friend, I struggle with regret over what occurred that day in the drop-off line.

Of course, I couldn't foresee that over time I would feel remorse over my decision to help Carly shut down her seeing gift.

In the moment, following a long season of confusion and struggles in our home, I honestly was desperate for a break. I'm sure you understand as you are likely staring this season in the face as well. However, what I didn't understand back then was this: shutting down her giftings resulted in a couple of consequences that I would undo today.

First, Carly no longer sees the heavenly angels, the "good angels." I miss hearing the stories from her visions in the heavenly realm.

Second, Carly, actually all of my children, have been spiritually gifted by God since they were babies. And now that I've gained a greater appreciation for each gift, I understand they are incredibly useful when a person works within their ability by asking good questions of Jesus.

Now that Carly no longer perceives the demons, we don't always know when they are present and interfering with our lives. When she turned off her seeing gift, she began to "feel" the spirit realm around her. She experienced several mood swings because she was affected by the demonic that she could no longer see but only feel. It left her, all of us, at a disadvantage.

The enemies of God prefer to remain invisible and undetected. This is especially true because they risk being dispatched back to the pit.

Seeing and revealing the enemy is half the battle. Consequently, I impaired my little girl that day when I helped her shut down her seeing gift. With that stated, Jesus was there, and out of his great compassion, offered a way forward. And because the gifts are irrevocable by God, I refuse to believe that her gifting is gone forever.

Yet if he (the enemy) is caught, he must pay sevenfold, though it costs him all the wealth of his house.
PROVERBS 6:31

Today, I'm standing in faith and claiming that the demonic must pay back what he stole from our family, seven times over in blessings, gifts, anointings, mandates, and more. As a family we stand in agreement with God's Word. The fact that Jesus was present in the moment as a witness affords me tremendous hope for Carly's complete and full restoration of her spiritual sight, plus some. And not only that, but she will also possess understanding and discernment enabling her to effectively use her gifts to help others.

I believe her restoration is in process and she will step fully into adulthood equipped with an enormous spiritual tool belt that multiplies and releases spiritual awareness and the gifts of heaven to others. It's my prayer that she exercises her gifts on earth to glorify Jesus.

Simple next step: Understand that fear is real but becomes powerless in the light of love and truth of Jesus.

Also, remember to love and forgive yourself for choices made in the past. And ask Jesus for his help and forgiveness throughout this process.

5

OPERATING IN THE GIFTS OF HEAVEN

Lynn

For God's gifts and his call are irrevocable.
ROMANS 11:29

The gifts of God are irrevocable. However, we have learned that out of sheer desperation, an individual may exercise their free will and shut down their spiritual discernment. For some, this single decision echoes with a lifetime of consequence, as spiritual sight is rendered dormant. Shutting off the gift offers a limited respite from the childhood drama, but at the same time there exists the potential that the child is handicapped for years, even a lifetime.

God provides unique gifts for each of us. When our gifting is exerted within the bounds of the Kingdom of God, we live out of God's fullness and contentment. Spiritual gifts offer us protection, discernment, love, and greater awareness of our true purpose. Supernatural gifts are designed to connect us intimately with God and are intended to serve people. These gifts are tremendously beneficial to those who work within them, and when they are combined with Godly wisdom and understanding, our daily lives are enhanced.

Allow me to provide a personal example that demonstrates a gift implemented as intended.

I pray with people who live all around the world. A portion of my ministry is dedicated to Healing Prayer. These are two-hour prayer sessions over the phone that are designed to connect people to Jesus. The prayee and I seek his voice and ask him questions. We allow the love and the presence of God to heal trauma, soul wounds, physical illness, and much more.

I'm privileged to spend two hours with an individual and participate as Jesus restores what the enemy has stolen. Within these sessions, I use my gift of discernment. I also lean into the gift, words of knowledge and work in a prophetic gifting.

I've developed a strong ability to discern the spiritual realm. I've engaged this gift through my personal faith, devotion, and seeking to restore all the gifts that were taken from me as a child. I'll explain more about that in the next chapter. But for now I want to share how a prayer session plays out when I engage my gifting.

I am a hearer. This is my main sensory gift. I listen to Jesus and he equips me with specific prayer strategies for the individual for whom I'm praying. Through my hearing gift, Jesus speaks into my mind, knowledge, divine wisdom, and specifics which helps the prayee to connect to his love, healing, and deliverance.

I recall a specific prayer session which remains a treasured memory. I began to pray with a young woman, age 20. Fresh from rehab, she was seeking freedom from dark thoughts, addictions, and past experiences. She shared that up until just recently, she was a practicing witch who was involved in blood majik. This is evil, dark, and demonic stuff.

My prayer partner, Deb, started the prayer session, and as she prayed, I began to discern the Lord's voice. I clearly discerned Jesus say to me, "She needs to pray the prayer of salvation."

So I asked this beautiful young woman, "Connie (not her name), have you prayed and asked Jesus into your heart?"

"I don't know. I'm not sure."

"Would you like to?"

"Yes, let's do it."

Deb proceeded to lead her through a simple prayer of salvation. What happened next was out of this world.

Immediately upon praying, the entire room suddenly filled with the love of God. The atmosphere charged. It electrified. The love of our Father rushed into the room, wave upon wave. All of us were experiencing the tangible love and presence of God.

Holy goose bumps traveled all over my body, then hit Deb and overwhelmed Connie. "This is amazing," I shouted. Deb was all smiles and agreement.

Connie looked stunned, happy, and overwhelmed, in a good way. She shouted, "What is happening?!? THIS IS AMAZING!"

"Connie, this is the love of God. He has been waiting for you all of your life. He is so happy you chose him today."

We went on to have the most amazing prayer session. That young woman was set free from tremendous evil. I watched her walk out of the Kingdom of darkness and into the Kingdom of light.

It was magnificent.

This supernatural moment became possible because I discerned the voice of God. If it wasn't for the Lord's voice speaking to me, I might have missed Connie's moment to pray the salvation prayer. And that prayer was exactly what was needed that day.

SUPERNATURAL GIFTS: FAITH, DISCERNMENT, PRAYER

Lynn

No, in all these things we are more than conquerors through him who loved us. For I am convinced that neither death nor life, neither angels nor demons, neither the present nor the future, nor any powers, neither height nor depth, nor anything else in all creation, will be able to separate us from the love of God that is in Christ Jesus our Lord.
ROMANS 8:37-39

That afternoon, praying for Connie, I engaged in direct conversation with Jesus. The Father, Jesus, and the Holy Spirit were listening and waiting. When I pray and tune into this gifting, I feel God's love, his approval, and an intimacy which rewards my soul. I am operating out of a Godly design.

Connie encountered the Trinity. All three of the Godhead arrived and revealed their delight in her, their love and power.

Often people live out their entire lives without a direct encounter with God. This should not be! We are invited to engage and hear our Shepherd's voice.

Jesus said: My sheep listen to my voice; I know them, and they follow me.
JOHN 10:27

I've found that a two-hour prayer session heals a person of tremendous trauma. Prayer releases them from lies, unforgiveness, and frees them from oppression. For many, the benefits of a two-hour prayer session often surpasses the gains of a year of traditional counseling.

I believe in counseling. And I believe in prayer. Both are effective, but I have witnessed time and again the powerful healing that occurs when Jesus shows up with his love, truth, authority, and his blood. Hallelujah!

The challenge is this: once a gift is snuffed out, it's difficult to reignite it and sometimes it never returns. However, with intentional effort and some training, spiritual gifting is likely to resume, even though, in my experience, it's never as strong or as easy as it was when a child retains the gift into adulthood.

As parents when we steward our child's gifts from a place of truth and love and away from fear, we are offering our kids tremendous potential, dignity, and a fulfilling purpose in their adult life.

In the Bible we read about people who possess powerful gifts. But the greatest examples of gifts are found in the earthly life of Jesus Christ. The first four books of the New Testament retell the many accounts of Jesus performing miracles and how he engaged through intimacy with our Father in heaven to operate in various gifts.

The New Testament is brimming with the supernatural. The accounts of divine gifts are contained throughout the Bible. They are recorded as examples for us to study, apprehend, then apply to our lives. God offers every human gifts. But there is a catch. God is looking for people to walk with him in intimacy, and develop into mature, responsible sons and daughters of the Kingdom. God bestows greater power and authority through gifts when we demonstrate love, restraint, and wisdom. He's looking for sons and daughters that will hold back from using our gifting for selfish gain or from immature faith that could potentially harm ourselves or others.

Increasing giftedness is derived from our commitment to living in faith and intimacy with the Trinity.

Now that we have explored several real-life supernatural gifts, let's take a look at a number of gifts that Annie and I find are common in the Kingdom of God.

6

SPIRITUAL GIFTS

Lynn

Now about the gifts of the Spirit, brothers and sisters, I do not want you to be uninformed.

1 CORINTHIANS 12:1

There are a number of spiritual gifts. They are below with scripture references:

- Faith (1 Corinthians 12:9)
- Giving (Romans 12:8)
- Hospitality (Romans 12:13)
- Kindness (Romans 12:8)
- Knowledge (1 Corinthians 12:8)
- Leadership (Romans 12:8)
- Pastor/Shepherding (Ephesians 4:11)
- Prophecy/Perceiving (Romans 12:6, 1 Corinthians 12:10)
- Teaching (Romans 12:7, 1 Corinthians 12:28, Ephesians 4:11)
- Serving/Ministry (Romans 12:7)
- Mercy (Romans 12:8)
- Wisdom (1 Corinthians 12:8)
- Gift of healing (1 Corinthians 12:9)

- Miracles (1 Corinthians 12:10)
- Tongues (1 Corinthians 12:10)
- Interpretation of tongues (1 Corinthians 12:10)

The Apostle Paul offers us insight into the gifts of the Spirit.

Now about the gifts of the Spirit, brothers and sisters, I do not want you to be uninformed...There are different kinds of gifts, but the same Spirit distributes them. There are different kinds of service, but the same Lord. There are different kinds of working, but in all of them and in everyone it is the same God at work.
Now to each one the manifestation of the Spirit is given for the common good. To one there is given through the Spirit a message of wisdom, to another a message of knowledge by means of the same Spirit, to another faith by the same Spirit, to another gifts of healing by that one Spirit, to another miraculous powers, to another prophecy, to another distinguishing between spirits, to another speaking in different kinds of tongues, and to still another the interpretation of tongues. All these are the work of one and the same Spirit, and he distributes them to each one, just as he determines.
1 CORINTHIANS 12:1-11

In this passage it's clear that spiritual gifts are bestowed by God to people. In my years of experience, I've discovered that generally people learn, practice, then participate in a number of gift sets depending upon the situation at hand. It's fascinating that specific gifts will function with nuances that are as individual as people. For example, some see angels, some hear them. This variation is dependent on the person's unique gift of perception.

Commonly the spiritual is perceived through one of the five senses. In addition to our senses, many recognize the spiritual through their faith. A person may function in all of these senses, but most are inclined to operate with a primary or dominate sense.

Let's discuss the five senses: sight, hearing, touch, smell, and taste.

THE SEER GIFT

Lynn

When the servant of the man of God got up and went out early the next morning, an army with horses and chariots had surrounded the city. "Oh no, my lord! What shall we do?" the servant asked.
"Don't be afraid," the prophet answered. "Those who are with us are more than those who are with them."
And Elisha prayed, "Open his eyes, Lord, so that he may see." Then the Lord opened the servant's eyes, and he looked and saw the hills full of horses and chariots of fire all around Elisha.
2 KINGS 6:15-17

This passage reveals Elisha, the teacher, asking God to open the spiritual eyes of his servant, thus enabling him to view the angels positioned to strike the enemies of God.

This is an example of an individual receiving spiritual sight. Spiritual vision will function in various degrees or capacities from person-to-person.

Some individuals, such as Carly, peer into the spiritual realm with their natural eyes and see spiritual reality with clarity. However, seers are also perceiving the spiritual through their spiritual sight at the same time. Carly would look with her natural eyes and see angels. But there are many who see into the spiritual through their mind. An image is reflected onto their "heart/mind" and they perceive a picture.

This is a seer gift. The seer will see or perceive images of the spiritual world that surrounds them. Some have a greater ability, such as viewing future events when exercising the prophetic in concert with their seeing gift. When they see angels and demons, they are also discerning spirits, which is another spiritual gift.

A seer will primarily view the spiritual realm through their eyes, spiritual and/or physical. They may also function in any other realm such as hearing, touch, etc.

THE HEARER

Lynn

Then the Lord called Samuel.
Samuel answered, "Here I am." And he ran to Eli and said, "Here I am; you
called me."
But Eli said, "I did not call; go back and lie down." So he went and lay
down.
Again the Lord called, "Samuel!" And Samuel got up and went to Eli and
said, "Here I am; you called me."
"My son," Eli said, "I did not call; go back and lie down."
Now Samuel did not yet know the Lord: The word of the Lord had not yet
been revealed to him.
A third time the Lord called, "Samuel!" And Samuel got up and went to Eli
and said, "Here I am; you called me."
Then Eli realized that the Lord was calling the boy. So Eli told Samuel,
"Go and lie down, and if he calls you, say, 'Speak, Lord, for your servant is
listening.'" So Samuel went and lay down in his place.
The Lord came and stood there, calling as at the other times, "Samuel!
Samuel!"
Then Samuel said, "Speak, for your servant is listening."
1 SAMUEL 3:4-10

In this passage the young temple assistant, Samuel, hears God's voice. He hears and responds by running to the familiar voice of the High Priest. Finally, the boy lies down and answers God, "Speak, for your servant is listening."

Samuel's belief and obedience opens a lifelong conversation between himself and God.

When an individual operates primarily through the gift of hearing, they experience audible sound, or more commonly, most people hear internally. A few common examples are the singing of angels, music, nature sounds, or the clanging of swords, and they perceive the voice of God. There are also a number who hear demonic voices and other sounds from the dark realm.

My primary sensory gift is hearing. I'm an internal hearer so what I perceive or "hear" within the spirit realm is mainly accomplished by listening with my mind/heart which are my spiritual ears. I exercise this gift when in prayer. I tune into the heart of God and listen for his voice. I also practice honing my hearing ability. It's an intentional, purposeful engaging of my will to focus and listen to what the Lord is speaking. I exercise my faith, my will, and my primary spiritual gift. And all of this gifting is possible because I am intentional to remain in an intimate relationship with God.

Early on, as I was redeveloping my spiritual hearing, I recall sitting around the fire pit in the backyard on a summer morning. I was reading my Bible around nine in the morning when suddenly a delightful four-stringed quartet composition drifted over the fence above my head and into the surrounding garden. I'll tell you this, it was impossible for there to be stringed music in my garden at nine a.m. And within a minute the beautiful melody floated away on the morning breeze.

Within that experience I felt the love and great pleasure of the Lord. And I hold that experience as a treasure within my heart. It was heavenly.

There are people who will hear the spiritual realm audibly with their natural ears. I recall a friend of mine recounting her salvation

MY CHILD SEES MONSTERS

story. She was enrolled in a religion class in college. Feeling confused with the number of religions discussed in class, she sat out under a tree one afternoon and out of sheer frustration blurted out, "What is the truth?"

Immediately an audible voice responded, "I am the Lord Jesus Christ. Follow me." I asked her what the voice sounded like. She replied, "Rushing waters." I'm not sure what that may sound like, however, that single moment redirected her entire life. She went from atheist to a pastor and a woman sold out for Christ.

Pray this passage back to the Lord often. It is our invitation into the hearing gift.

My sheep listen to my voice; I know them, and they follow me.
JOHN 10:27

THE GIFT OF SCENT & TASTE

Lynn

*So God created mankind in his own image, in the image of God he created
them; male and female he created them.*
GENESIS 1:27

There are those who smell fragrances in the spiritual realm. I
know that I've picked up on the scent of roses while in worship.
There are those who can smell something like fire and brimstone,
acrid smoke and burning sulfur (rotten eggs). These unpleasant
aromas are indicators that a foul spirit is about. Just as in the
natural, it's possible to discern the spiritual realm through smell.

This is a particularly pleasant sensibility when joined with faith
and devotion to our Father in heaven. God designed us in his
image (Genesis 1:27). He created our senses that we would enjoy
his creation of beauty, sound, sight, and smell. I find this specific
gift offers us joy and wonder.

In contrast, this gift also operates as a warning. Detecting a
smell that comes out of the pit is a telltale sign that a demonic
presence is at hand.

The gift of taste operates similarly to the gifting of scent. It
offers the individual a specific avenue to discern the spiritual realm

through their sense of taste. Smell and taste are closely linked. Often you smell and taste at the same time. It's a heightened awareness and confirmation of the spiritual surroundings.

THE KNOWER GIFT

Lynn

*When **Jesus perceived their thoughts**, he answered them, "Why do
you question in your hearts?" ESV*
LUKE 5:22

We make hundreds of choices every day. We engage our free will to
choose right over wrong, love over fear — a salad over cheese fries.
Our free will is extraordinarily powerful. Our entire experience on
earth ultimately concerns our free will and the choices we make on
earth as well as our choice for eternity.

The perceiver/knower gift is born of our free will and our faith
(belief) and this function of the spiritual gifts is tremendous. This
gift arises out of desire. Spiritual perception is apprehended
through surrender to God and the continual practice of his principles and precepts, intimacy. It is possible to develop spiritual
senses when we engage our will with perseverance asking the Lord
for this gifting.

I've mentioned before that as a child, I shut down all of my
spiritual gifts. But in my adult years, I began to pursue the reawakening or apprehending the gifts of the Spirit. Because I lost my
spiritual senses, I leaned completely on my faith and I chose every

day to believe I would pick up a gift of miracles as well as a prophetic hearing gift. I was determined to hear my Lord's voice.

With fervor I prayed scriptures that affirmed the gifts and asked Jesus to reawaken spiritual abilities within. I would seek understanding by reading the Bible and other books that offered Biblical teaching and then I would pray, pray, pray and practice, practice, practice.

I actively willed my reawakening. Today my hearing gift continues to increase in levels of effectiveness because I pray, practice, and believe.

Listening with my "heart" through my perceiving gift, I've gained the ability to discern spirits. I receive words of knowledge and there are times I just know things. I know in my mind information or receive intuition about situations, atmospheres, people, etc. My knower gift led to my hearing gift and today my seeing ability is sharpening.

The spiritual gifts I walk in today were born out of my great desire to pursue God. I determined my will to this passage:

Ask and it will be given to you; seek and you will find; knock and the door will be opened to you. For everyone who asks receives; the one who seeks finds; and to the one who knocks, the door will be opened.
MATTHEW 7:7-8

This is love. God loves us and when we pursue him, he lavishes his love, presence, and his gifts. He is a generous Father.

TOUCH OR FEELER GIFT

Lynn

But solid food is for the mature, for those who have their powers of discernment trained by constant practice to distinguish good from evil.
HEBREWS 5:14 ESV

One of the supernatural gifts is somewhat difficult to describe. People will "feel" the spiritual realm in various and differing capacities. Some physically feel a spiritual manifestation such as oil pouring on their heads in worship and the presence of God. Or from the dark realm, scratches on their body or pressure on their chest at night while sleeping are a few examples. Others feel the atmosphere of the room. Still others perceive and vividly experience the strong emotions of another when in close proximity.

When Carly's seeing gift shut down, her secondary gifting, feeling, was accentuated. She could perceive fear and terror but no longer could see the beings that were near her. This is true for many who will sense the spiritual.

I'll share a common example that I encounter through my Spiritual Development Coaching ministry. When working with a client to develop their spiritual gifts, I'll ask them if they have struggled with depression or a sense of foreboding. I'll ask them if it's common to walk into a room and abruptly feel sad or even a sense of suicide. I'll follow with a few more questions to discern whether their strong emotions are rooted within themselves or if they are picking up on emotions or feeling the emotions of others around them. When I determine depression isn't rooted in their own pain, I begin to explain how they are likely operating out of a "feeling gift" in the spirit.

I'll handle that session something like this.

"Do you walk into a room and within a few minutes start to feel anxious, sad, or depressed?

A typical answer, "Yes. This does happen to me."

"Do you feel confused as to why you are feeling these emotions as you weren't sad, depressed, or anxious a minute earlier?"

"Yes. It's very confusing and has been for a long time!"

I proceed to explain what they are experiencing is the spiritual realm. They feel/sense/perceive the strong emotions of those in the room and/or spirits in the room. I affirm that they are a spiritual feeler and when they pick up on emotions, they are functioning in a perception gift from God.

I'll ask, "Have you struggled with intermittent depression, anxiety, and fear for years?"

Typically, the individual will respond yes. With a few more questions we determine if this gift has been with them since childhood.

This is the moment I share the liberating information they've needed since they were a child. "You've believed these confusing emotions belonged to you even when there wasn't a solid reason behind these feelings."

Once I share this truth with them, it's as though a lifetime of confusion and oppression falls away. They feel a tremendous relief to finally have an explanation for their wild emotions.

And the best part of this conversation is I provide them with tools, when learned, help them to function in their gifting for their benefit and the benefit of others.

My dear friend, would you like to possess these tools as well? Here they are.

When sensing emotions that appear suddenly or appear contrary to your own, ask Jesus three questions. Pray them in your mind and listen to his reply.

First question: Jesus, what is happening here?

Listen for his reply.

For example. He will respond with vital information. He may reply indicating a spirit of death or suicide is near. Or perhaps there is a spirit of depression or that witchcraft is at work in the room.

Listening is critical. Gaining understanding extends insight into what is next.

Question two: Jesus, who is it?

If you look about the room, typically a person becomes highlighted. You will have a knowing about the specific individual. It takes time to learn how to discern whom Jesus is highlighting. But ask and continue to ask as this process sharpens your spirit and gifting. Jesus will sometimes share a name, or your gaze will come to rest on the person. And if you concentrate and listen, what happens next is a knowing will occur in your spirit. You will just know. I call this a holy download.

Information is given to help guide you to speak or pray. And if no one is highlighted continue on to the next question.

Question three: Jesus, what do you want me to do?

This is a time to press in and focus on his still small voice speaking to your heart/mind. Jesus will reveal his desire in the situation. Sometimes he merely wants you to pray. He may ask you to pray, commanding the evil spirit you are sensing, such as the spirit of death and suicide, to leave.

There are times he'll want you to bless the room/person with the opposite spirit. Bless with hope, joy, peace, resurrection life. In Jesus' name. Always in Jesus' name.

Or at times, he will ask you to initiate a conversation with the highlighted individual with the intent to lead into a moment where you share and pray. I find this happens when Jesus knows the individual is receptive. Jesus always has a tremendous desire to free humanity from the oppressor.

My experience is that Jesus will ask us for interaction in a manner we are capable and comfortable with. Well, most of the time. He knows how much spiritual authority we carry and he also understands our courage level. However, there are moments he will urge us forward with brave steps as he's desperate to help someone. His love is relentless and urges us to take up courage and follow his voice with obedience. He works through us, as he is compelled to release people from demonic strongholds.

Three simple questions to apply to every spiritual gift:

1. Jesus, what is happening?
2. Jesus, who is it?
3. Jesus, what do you want me to do?

Once I've shared these simple steps with those who are feelers, their lives are changed. First, they no longer are burdened by the emotions that belong to others. Secondly, they possess powerful tools that partner with Jesus to bring healing and hope into their lives and the lives of those around them.

These steps are applicable to all the gifts.

Take a brave step and use the gifts of God to help another person. Participating with Jesus as he touches a life with his love and healing changes you. You will experience his love, favor, joy, and wonder!

JOINING SPIRITUAL SENSES WITH SPIRITUAL GIFTS

Lynn

*To one there is given through the Spirit a message of wisdom, to another a
message of knowledge by means of the same Spirit.*
1 CORINTHIANS 12:8

Thus far, we've learned that combining our supernatural senses
with our spiritual gifting, opportunities will arise that literally
changes lives, releases healing, restores hope, and impacts our
world.

This concept is demonstrated in the Bible in the verse above.

A message of knowledge is also known as, *Words of Knowledge.*
The Holy Spirit informs an individual about a situation currently
at hand.

For me, I will exercise this gift when I'm in a prayer session.
Remember I'm a hearer. I listen as the Holy Spirit whispers a word
to me about the person for whom I'm praying. I might hear/per-
ceive some information such as the prayee is harboring unforgiveness.

This gift of knowledge prompts me to lead the prayee through
a forgiveness prayer. Jesus provides the cue that unforgiveness is
holding the person in chains of bitterness which are affecting their
spirit, soul, and ultimately their body.

Others, such as those with the feeler gifting, observe a sensation in their own body when the Lord is willing to heal the person for whom they are praying. I watched this happen recently. A woman suddenly felt pain in her calf. She asked the person for whom she was praying if she was experiencing pain in her calf.

Yes, was the immediate answer.

The woman leading the prayer proceeded to command all the pain to leave and blessed the suffering woman with healing from Jesus. The pain immediately left. The woman who was leading the prayer discerned a signal from God through a sensation of touch.

Both of these examples are the workings of Words of Knowledge, but they are expressed differently through the individual based upon their primary spiritual gifting (sense).

Spiritual gifts are stepping stones which lead us into greater realms of identity, authority and a victorious Kingdom life. Now that we have gained a general understanding of spiritual gifts, it's time to learn our authority in Christ. Spiritual gifts are intended to bring Kingdom benefits to humanity and our gifting becomes extraordinary and powerful when combined with spiritual authority.

1

TWO SIMPLE STEPS TO VICTORY

Ann Marie

Overwhelming victory is ours through Christ, who loved us.
ROMANS 8:37b NLT

While traveling along this dusty path, learning to understand the spiritual realm, I met Lynn Donovan at church. She and I connected through the ministry school on campus. She was an instructor of one of the courses and from there we became fast friends. The courses at church equipped me to grow in spiritual authority. I acquired my true strength and influence through Jesus Christ.

I recall an evening in class when a powerful segment regarding cleansing was presented. I discovered I could check my kids' rooms for anything that might have a demonic attachment. I learned how witchcraft, hexes, and curses might attach to toys, stuffed animals, or any object for that matter. I also learned how to discern what and where open doors to the demonic realm might exist in my home which allowed entry of a demon. It was during this season that Lynn taught me how to take authority over my home.

Previously, I shared that praying for Carly tremendously changed our home; however, a number of years later she began avoiding her room once again, except to retrieve her clothing. She refused to step across the threshold unless a family member was a protective escort.

However, things were different this time. I was no longer ignorant of the devil's schemes and I'd gained momentum and received some helpful advice from Lynn and a few of the other leaders of our congregation. One immensely helpful suggestion was to rid our life, home, and family of evil influence.

One day I decided to take their advice. I waited until no one was at home and armed myself with just enough information and a tiny bit of faith.

I started this epic and unprecedented adventure by opening every door and window in the entire house, as recommended by Lynn. Next, I grabbed my essential oil, blessing it in Jesus' name, and then sat down silently on the floor, one room at a time. I invited the Holy Spirit into the room. I prayed, asking the Holy Spirit if there was anything that was unholy or that opposed the love of Jesus. In each room I discerned a picture or heard a word in my head identifying something in the room that was not right. I picked it up, threw it out, and then recited this prayer:

Father, I come boldly and confidently into your presence and I stand in authority in this house and in this room. I now cast out any demonic thing or activity that is not of you. I send it to the foot of the cross. It cannot return, nor retaliate against me or my family members. It can't ask for help on the way out. In Jesus' mighty name.

Then I blessed each room with family unity, good communication, bold conversations, love, and anything more I sensed was needed and always in the name of Jesus.

I arrived at my boys' room. I proceeded to bless it and then bless them by name with purity, healthy thoughts, a good relationship with Christ Jesus, and anything additional that the Lord brought to mind.

In my bedroom, I blessed my husband and myself with a deep connection with Christ as the center of our lives. I blessed us with pure hearts as I touched my oil-covered finger above each window and door frame. Then I requested a protecting angel be stationed at each window and door, with swords drawn, and commanded them to lop off each demonic head that dared to enter.

Yay, fun times!

Finally, I arrived at Carly's room. I saved that room for last.

I decided to lay on her bed, and as I did, I heard a nasty little voice, "You don't know what you're doing. You're not nearly strong enough to do this. You don't carry authority and I'm not leaving."

I was only mildly surprised by this foul spirit's threats but wasn't frightened. Not in the least. In fact, I was mad! I began to pray, asking the Holy Spirit to alert me to any toys, books, or stuffed animals which might carry a curse or anything not of God. I discovered a piano book in her toy box. Wouldn't you know it, the book contained a Halloween song about witches, goblins, and ghouls. I tossed it. Next, I found a Magic 8-Ball, which I also tossed, and finally a few stuffed animals that my mom purchased from a yard sale.

After everything was dispatched to the trash, I returned, armed with conviction and a growing strength in faith. I commanded, out loud and in a forceful voice: *Anything not of God, I dispatch you immediately to the foot of the cross.*

Throughout this entire process, the nasty evil spirit remained upon the bed spewing lies. For a minute I entertained confusion. But that passed and then I was armed with a new thought. *Bless her room.* With conviction, I blessed my daughter with purity, love, joy, happiness. Finally, I realized a powerful word was rising from deep within and I yelled at the top of my lungs: *FEAR-LESSNESS!*

Instantly a powerful gust of wind whooshed in through the window. The oil diffuser flew off her dresser and spilled on the floor. The wind roughly pushed past me, passed through Carly's door, then exited the house through the front door.

The door slammed shut with a violent force!

I stood in utter shock, mouth hanging open. I gained my composure and closed my lips then turned around slowly noticing something shifted. A new and beautiful peace filled our home. And that nasty little voice disappeared. Praise God!

What an experience. I cried my eyes out when I realized what just happened.

I laid down on the living room floor, exhausted but peaceful, staring at the front door that slammed shut.

Within minutes the family began arriving home from school and work. I stood up as Carly came in. She offered a hug and pecked my cheek, then proceeded to the bathroom. I covertly watched as she walked down the hall past her bedroom. She offered a quick glance inside, then stopped in her tracks, backed up a few paces, and took a long second look. Next, she cautiously stuck her head in past the door frame, then stepped all the way inside.

I watched her carefully examine the room. And within about thirty seconds I could hear her giggles as she jumped up and down on the bed! She knew what I knew. That nasty little spirit was gone. For some reason, we never spoke about what happened that day. I wish we had.

What a day! What an experience! My mind was blown! God confirmed through the slamming of the door on that nasty beast that my prayers and declarations were working!

RESTORING JOY, PEACE, TRUST, AND COMMUNICATION: CLOSING THE DOORS

Ann Marie

For the kingdom of God is not eating and drinking, but righteousness and peace and joy in the Holy Spirit.
ROMANS 14:17

Learning to take authority through Christ over the demonic was a powerful lesson in that season. It changed my life and that of my family. I went on to toss things out with every single attack and by the prompting of the Holy Spirit, over and again with frequency. I became absolutely determined to free our home and children. I would not relent.

In this season I experienced a dramatic dream. Dreams are also significant in the spiritual realm. They are another form of spiritual gifting. In the dream an enormous, dark hole opened in the ceiling of my bedroom. A large, thick blanket emerged, lowered, then covered me. I couldn't breathe and instantly I felt some sort of disgusting perversion. I woke immediately, deeply disturbed in my spirit. Instantly I knew in my knower that I must check on the boys.

It was early in the morning hours as I tiptoed down the hall. Sleeping bags carpeted the floor of the family room. The place was overrun by neighborhood boys, invited to a slumber party with my son. I expected the kids to finally be crashed out as I quietly stepped into the mess. Interestingly, I noticed one of the boys was awake. When he spotted me, he quickly hid the screen of his phone, tucking it under the flap of his sleeping bag and feigned sleep. As I hovered in the room, I discerned something perverse and unclean was upon that boy's screen. I knew immediately this was the open door that birthed my bizarre and disturbing dream.

This time, I knew exactly what to do. I quietly took authority under my breath. With my prayer, I placed a blanket of purity and restful sleep over all the boys. Upon finishing my prayer, I felt peaceful and returned to bed feeling satisfied that I recognized the opening and I KNEW how to shut this open door.

What is interesting is that although I'd discovered many sources of entry of foul spirits into my home and also how to successfully shut open doors, I'm not always able to permanently close off doors in the spiritual. The reality is that we live with family members who have free will. Their choices often affect the spiritual climate of our home.

From that day forward, I became proactive instead of responding from a defensive posture. I started to teach my boys about their choices and actions and how they impact their sister. They also experienced the result of her spiritual visions and felt compassion over her suffering. I leaned into their love. They agreed they would do anything to protect her. I explained the real possibility that the content they watched on their phones during the day, but especially right before bed, created an open door for the enemy.

Initially, they pushed back as they didn't believe what they were viewing was "that bad." I explained that it didn't matter if what they saw was harmless for them, what mattered in our home was how it opens a door.

One of them fired back a great question. "Mom, if watching stuff on the phone, television, or a gaming console created an open door for the enemy, why aren't we affected?"

I continued, "Your sister sees in the spirit. Please think twice about what you are watching." Understanding brought about their agreement for Carly's sake and peace for all of us.

Following our conversation, the demonic activity slowed, but didn't entirely disappear. When Carly had another active, draining night, in the nicest and most loving way possible, I quizzed the boys about what they watched on their phones the prior evening. Their faces revealed the truth.

They knew their actions precipitated another rough night for their sister, as it opened a door. I never shamed the boys, but was intentional to help them to understand the consequences which impacted our home.

Stepping into my authority through Christ and closing the open doors to the demonic was pivotal for all of us, especially Carly. And when Carly was at peace, so were the rest of us.

SIMPLE STEPS INTO SPIRITUAL AUTHORITY

Ann Marie

Calling the Twelve to him, he began to send them out two by two and gave them authority over impure spirits.

MARK 6:7

A few years ago as I was climbing into bed, I heard Carly scream bloody murder from her room. Both feet hit the floor as I bolted toward the shrieking. Before I could get through the bedroom door, she rushed in and threw herself into my arms. Her hands covered her face as she cried-screamed, "Help me!"

"What's wrong? What happened?" I tried to remain calm and gently pried her hands from her eyes.

"It's a demon in my face. And when I close my eyes he's still there!"

"Okay, we know what to do." I summoned my courage and the wisdom I'd gained. "Do you remember what we learned from Jennifer Toledo's book?"

"Yes, Mom. Will you help me?"

"Of course. Climb up on the bed." I patted the bed. She scrambled up and sat down. She was breathing rapidly as her eyes darted frantically about the room.

"Take a deep breath, Carly."

I heard her inhale then exhale slowly, but panic quickly set in again.

"Not today, Satan!" I spoke firmly and with authority into the spiritual realm. "I command you to go, in Jesus' name. You cannot come back, retaliate, or ask for help on your way out! GO!"

"Carly, do you know its name or where it came from?"

"NO!" Tearily, "But it was scary."

"Okay, let's do this. Close your eyes. Okay? Now, let me know when you can see the white dry-erase board in your head." We learned this technique a few months earlier from the Toledo book.

"Yes, I see it and the demon is on it!"

"Okay, try to remain calm and repeat after me. Father, God, please show me where you are."

"He is here, Mom! He's with me."

"Okay, that's good. Ask him to erase the demon from the whiteboard." She breathed in a big sigh of relief and let me know the demon was erased.

"Okay, now let's thank him for doing that. Thank you, Lord."

"Thank you, Lord," she repeats.

"Now ask him to draw you a new picture on the whiteboard."

"Okay, it's peaceful."

"Good, now ask him where the demon came from."

"Tennis practice?" I could hear the surprise in her voice.

"What happened at tennis?"

"Well, my friend shared with me that her school teacher required the class to write a horror story for Halloween. She told me all about what she wrote. It was pretty scary."

"Okay, let's ask God for forgiveness for opening that door and let's ask him to seal it shut. Finally let's ask him if there is anything more we need to do."

"Yes, I need to pray for my friend and especially the teacher."

"Okay, would you like my help praying for them?"

"No Mom, it's okay. I've got this. Thanks, Mom." She hugged me goodnight and returned to her room.

This recent encounter is remarkably familiar ground of the

terrors and fear our household experienced in years past. However, I've learned to take my authority in Christ and the outcome is an entirely different experience.

Additionally, this recent encounter confirms what I'd hoped— Carly's seeing gift remains. I believe she caught sight of the demon, creating a learning opportunity for her to put into practice what we've gained in the past few years. And perhaps this episode was for me to practice what I've learned as well.

I'm hopeful she will build on this experience to further her confidence, awareness, and expand her gifting. I'm convinced that when Carly partners her seeing gift with heaven, she will help a great number of people escape fear and oppression and step into true freedom.

SPIRITUAL AUTHORITY

Lynn

*Jesus said: I have given you authority to trample on snakes and scorpions
and to overcome all the power of the enemy; nothing will harm you.*
LUKE 10:19

Throughout this book Annie and I have shared examples of our
authority within the spiritual realm. Of course, we don't have
everything figured out and we continue to grow in our faith journey. Yet, we are convinced we are equipped through faith in Jesus
with enough basic knowledge of the spiritual to attain a level of
authority that protects and aids our children. Our homes become a
place of love, peace, and a place of refuge for ourselves, our kids,
and others.

The first simple step into authority begins with the belief that
through the love of Christ you have his authority to send away the
demonic. Salvation plus simple faith. These are powerful steps to
defeat fear and the darkness.

When Annie's children were small, she carried a minimal
amount of knowledge. However, she chose to believe her children's
experiences. She also chose to have confidence in what she knew
about the Kingdom of light and the love of Christ. Her tiny faith
and authority proved enough in the moment.

Do not fear! This message is repeated over and over in the Bible, 365 times, once for every day of the year. We have nothing to fear from evil spirits. In fact, the demons are terrified you are reading this book and discovering your power over them. They know defeat is near at hand.

We overcome the work of the devil when we believe the scriptures and follow the examples and teaching of Jesus. Let's take a look at our authority through Christ.

*When Jesus had called the Twelve together, **he gave them power and authority to drive out all demons and** to cure diseases, and he sent them out to proclaim the kingdom of God and to heal the sick.*
LUKE 9:1-2

*Jesus said: **I have given you authority** to trample on snakes and scorpions and to overcome all the power of the enemy; nothing will harm you.*
LUKE 10:19

Authority begins with a simple choice. When we choose to believe what is in the Word of God we will receive authority as a disciple of Christ over ALL the works of the enemy. One simple step. Start with FAITH. Then pursue God with all that you are.

Now faith is the substance of things hoped for, the evidence of things not seen.
HEBREWS 11:1

PERSONAL CHARACTER AND FAITH

Lynn

For this reason, since the day we heard about you, we have not stopped praying for you. We continually ask God to fill you with the knowledge of his will through all the wisdom and understanding that the Spirit gives, so that you may live a life worthy of the Lord and please him in every way: bearing fruit in every good work, growing in the knowledge of God.
COLOSSIANS 1:9-10

The depth in which you carry authority is directly tied to character quality, identity in Christ, and proportion of faith. The greater our faith and confidence in God, the greater our authority grows over the demons.

Begin your simple step of faith right now. Pray the salvation prayer located in the appendix of this book. Then practice the Simple Steps. Pick up the Bible and read the first five books of the New Testament. Example upon example of spiritual reality, authority, and triumph reside within these few short books. The Bible is an ageless text that offers humanity the blueprint for the highest and best life, victory, and a life of love and peace.

This all-time best seller brims with quality character traits, a message of love and acceptance, and provides examples of how

Jesus silenced demonic voices and activity. This book points us to hope, healing, and freedom.

Below is one such example where Jesus frees a child from demonic oppression. Let these words inspire and build your faith.

A man in the crowd answered, "Teacher, I brought you my son, who is possessed by a spirit that has robbed him of speech. Whenever it seizes him, it throws him to the ground. He foams at the mouth, gnashes his teeth and becomes rigid. I asked your disciples to drive out the spirit, but they could not."

"You unbelieving generation," Jesus replied, "how long shall I stay with you? How long shall I put up with you? Bring the boy to me."

So they brought him. When the spirit saw Jesus, it immediately threw the boy into a convulsion. He fell to the ground and rolled around, foaming at the mouth.

Jesus asked the boy's father, "How long has he been like this?"

"From childhood," he answered. "It has often thrown him into fire or water to kill him. But if you can do anything, take pity on us and help us."

"'If you can'?" said Jesus. "Everything is possible for one who believes."

Immediately the boy's father exclaimed, "I do believe; help me overcome my unbelief!"

When Jesus saw that a crowd was running to the scene, he rebuked the impure spirit. "You deaf and mute spirit," he said, "I command you, come out of him and never enter him again."

The spirit shrieked, convulsed him violently and came out. The boy looked so much like a corpse that many said, "He's dead." But Jesus took him by the hand and lifted him to his feet, and he stood up.

After Jesus had gone indoors, his disciples asked him privately, "Why couldn't we drive it out?"

He replied, "This kind can come out only by prayer."

MARK 9:17-29

Annie prayed a simple prayer one desperate night in her closet and it was enough. A simple command, demanding the spirit to leave in

Jesus' name. My friend, stand upon the scriptures. Read the Bible and believe the words. They are filled with truth and power.

In the book of Matthew Jesus adds to this story.

He replied, "Because you have so little faith. **Truly I tell you, if you have faith as small as a mustard seed, you can say to this mountain, 'Move from here to there,' and it will move. Nothing will be impossible for you."**
MATTHEW 17:20

A tiny seed. A mustard-seed-sized faith is our start-point to send the monsters away.

STEWARDING OUR CHILD'S GIFTS

Lynn

Three things will last forever—faith, hope, and love—and the greatest of these is love.
1 CORINTHIANS 13:13

LOVE.

This is the simplest step and the beginning of every successful endeavor in the Kingdom of God. Love releases our kids into a life of fulfillment and purpose. The love of Christ changes the world. Love propels us and our children into greater realms of wholehearted living.

It's our love for our family that will compel us to rise up against an unseen entity and speak commands, even if it feels foolish or frightening. It's love that matures our gifts. Love is the key. Love is central and eternal, and my friend, love is one of the few things that we take with us into the next life.

A powerful spiritual truth is this: We possess the highest authority over that which we love. Love guards our hearts so that we pray from a place of selflessness instead of selfishness. Loving your family, your home, your city, and nation compels the King of

ANN MARIE MORA & LYNN DONOVAN

the universe to lend you his ear. Our Father in heaven responds to love, then moves upon our prayers of faith because he is love.

Without love, the simple steps outlined in the book are merely words on a page. When we cross over into eternity, Jesus will ask every soul one question. Did you learn to love?

My friend, choose love.

Our life purpose is to learn one thing. Love well and thrive.

WHAT IS MY CHILD'S GIFTING?

Lynn

But the fruit of the Spirit is love, joy, peace, forbearance, kindness, goodness, faithfulness, gentleness and self-control.
GALATIANS 5:22-23a

To identify your child's gift set, begin with intentional listening and observation. Tune into what your child says. Watch them in play. When they ask questions, listen with purpose and don't offhandedly dismiss their childish prattling as make-believe. If they mention over and again that they hear voices or an imaginary friend chats with them, even at a young age, they may be hearing the supernatural realm. Over time look for consistency within their hints.

One simple step is to proactively ask your child questions. "Describe what you hear. Is it a voice, a sound? Scary or fun, bright or dark?"

From their answers you can determine if they hear audibly or through their mind. This active questioning technique is tremendously helpful to determine if your child hears audibly or perceiving in their spirit.

Does your child see things that you don't see? Ask them to describe what they see. Can they point to something in the room or are they perceiving it in the spirit, in their mind? Are they an external or internal seer?

If your child experiences mood swings when entering a new environment, they may be a feeler. Ask questions such as, "Tell me what is happening. How do you feel? Did you feel sad before we walked to the park?" All of these are great questions to ascertain when they are feeling their own emotions or the emotions of others or if they are perceiving spirits in the atmosphere.

Apply these similar questions to all the gifts. Also, consider what gifts that you, as a parent, possessed as a child. It's common that similar spiritual gifting travels family lines.

And finally, remember to affirm your child. Help them to understand that their gift doesn't make them wrong or bad. They need to know that they are loved and accepted and not perceived as something outside of normal.

CULTIVATING YOUR CHILD'S GIFT

Lynn

This is why I remind you to fan into flames the spiritual gift God gave you when I laid my hands on you.

2 TIMOTHY 1:6

As parents, we are positioned to shape and direct our child's spiritual gift. How do we steward a child's gifting? Empower and affirm your child. Then offer the gift back to God for his purposes. Here is a simple prayer that you and your child can pray together:

Jesus, you have given me a gift of _____ (name the gift). I thank you for trusting me with your gift. I promise to use it only for your purpose to help other people and myself to know you and grow closer to you. I choose to dedicate my spiritual gift to you forever. In your name, Jesus. Amen

Always remember to ask Jesus questions. Asking questions is the best way to remove the fear and gain insight into experiences.

Remember from chapter six we learned to ask three vital questions:

Jesus, what is going on here?'

Jesus, who is it?

Jesus, what do you want me to do?

To help your child learn from and process their encounter remember to ask Jesus, "What do you want me to learn from this?"

Teach your child the coping techniques. Annie directed Carly through her fear by using the whiteboard in her imagination.

Another effective tool is to ask Jesus, "Show me what the demon really looks like." Most evil spirits reflect a frightening image to intimidate, but Jesus will reveal they are often small, scrawny, and funny looking. You can also teach your child to shrink the demon, or as we learned earlier, simply command it away. Teaching your child their authority in the spiritual realm, is a life-long gift of great value.

Allow your child to hear you pray. When you demonstrate how to command the demons away, they learn and draw on that demonstration in times of stress when they can't lean on you. They carry these learned techniques into adulthood.

Let me ask you this. If your child became ill with a rare disease, wouldn't you take the initiative to study the research available from reputable sources? Do the same when learning about your child's spiritual abilities. Do your research. Be vigilant and discerning about the sources of your information. The internet is ablaze with a number of deceptive websites, as well as books, blog posts, etc. which lead down a path toward distortion and darkness. Seek out trusted sources written by well-known and seasoned people of faith in Jesus.

PROTECTING YOUR CHILD'S GIFT

Lynn

*Now about the gifts of the Spirit, brothers and sisters, I do not want you to
be uninformed.*
1 CORINTHIANS 12:1

Once the spiritual realm is closed off, for many it remains shut
down for a lifetime.

This is the endgame of the devil. He will do everything to
frighten and pervert what our child sees, hears, feels, and perceives
with the intention to shut off God and his gifts. However, by
taking a brave step of faith and using the simple steps in this book,
you offer your child a profound and extraordinary life. It's worth it.

My friend, we live in a world where there are a great number of
people who reject the reality of the spiritual realm and gifts from
heaven. The masses embrace deceptions that God, the spiritual
realm, and anything supernatural is the result of our imagination
or something yet to be explained by science. The western world is
conditioned into unbelief. Our society acclimatizes millions to
mock any expression of the spiritual.

Therefore, it's appropriate to tutor your child to know with
whom they are free to share their experiences. Sometimes it's

prudent to keep these amazing, yet little understood, gifts within the family. As Annie shared, her childrens' physician's approach was medication. And unfortunately, it's simply not understood even by a wide number in the Christian church today.

10

THERE IS HOPE AND HELP

Ann Marie

So humble yourselves before God. Resist the devil, and he will flee from you.
JAMES 4:7

"Dinner's ready!" I yelled while placing our hot meal on the table.

"Mom, where is Diggy going to sit?" Ben, my three-year-old, sulked.

"Oh, Diggy is eating with us tonight?" I played back. This wasn't a new request.

"Yep, he is."

"Okay, go get him a chair or he can just sit right next to you."

Halfway into dinner, Ben's full glass of milk flies across the table!

"What the?"

"Diggy, why'd you throw the milk?" Ben rushes with an excuse.

"Ben Michael! Go and get a rag. That was not cool."

"But it wasn't me. It was Diggy!"

"Okay, okay, just get the rag."

This was the common story in our house.

"Ben Michael, why did you make such a mess in your room?"

"I didn't. It was Diggy."

"Ben Michael, why is your brother's favorite Hot Wheels car in the toilet?

"Diggy threw it in there."

"Ugh, who threw a whole roll of toilet paper into the toilet?"

"I saw Diggy do it."

"What happened in the kitchen? Why is the cereal all over the floor?"

"I think Diggy was hungry."

"Ben Michael, that wasn't very kind. You hurt your brother with those words."

"Diggy told me to say it!" he cried regretfully.

My middle son, Ben, entertained this imaginary friend, Diggy, for a few years. Thankfully I believe I handled this particular spiritual encounter correctly, at least for the most part.

I played along, not because I believed Ben. I didn't. Not at all, but I'd recently read in a parenting magazine that imaginary friends will one day go away. I'm not sure about all that, but indeed, that is what happened in Ben's case.

I clearly recall Ben explaining that one day he woke up and knew that Diggy had to go. Ben stated, "I am stronger than him." So, on that day, he sent him on his way. It's interesting to me that Ben stood in his authority without any prior training or even any example of spiritual authority or prayer. Yet he recognized that Diggy wasn't a good character and led Ben into a great deal of trouble.

I'm amazed that Ben knew Diggy must go and he also knew instinctively how to send him away. This leads me to so much peace knowing how the Lord will help our kids even when we are unaware.

One of the things I would have liked to have asked Ben at the time was did he think Diggy loved him and cared about his well-being. I would have used an example of how his dad and I loved him so much that we made sure he was fed, had a bath, gave him good night kisses, and so on. Once Ben grasped that Diggy's intentions were mean and not helpful, I would have helped him with a simple prayer.

Father God, we come boldly and confidently into your presence today to thank you for the protection you provide over our home and our family. If Diggy does not love Ben or you, Lord, we command him to leave now. Send him to the foot of the cross. He must go where you tell him to go. Father, I place a holy ring of fire around our property and I command that protecting angels stand guard all around this ring of fire. Anything that is not of you cannot stay or penetrate through the ring. Thank you, Lord, for your angels and your continued protection. We ask all this in Jesus' mighty name. We love you, Father. Amen.

The simplicity of faith through our prayers changes our family and rescues our children from evil masquerading as a "friend."

BLESSING

Lynn

When an impure spirit comes out of a person, it goes through arid places seeking rest and does not find it. Then it says, 'I will return to the house I left.' When it arrives, it finds the house unoccupied, swept clean and put in order. Then it goes and takes with it seven other spirits more wicked than itself, and they go in and live there. And the final condition of that person is worse than the first. That is how it will be with this wicked generation.
MATTHEW 12:43-45

There is one vital step remaining that cannot be overlooked. In the book of Matthew, Jesus offers a profound insight into the demonic realm. The passage reveals that demons will leave but they will attempt to return.

With this reality in mind, we always want to fill up a person with a blessing. When we command a demonic entity to leave, follow up this moment with a blessing from Jesus. Jesus models blessings throughout the New Testament and specifically through the Sermon on the Mount (Matthew, chapter 5).

Simply praying a blessing creates a Kingdom atmosphere and fills your child with the attributes of heaven. For example, if your child was battling with fear and you command the fear to leave, pray first to thank Jesus for his goodness and for sending away the fear. Then pray and ask Jesus to bless your child with a spirit of peace, love, joy, hope, and a calm mind.

One of my favorite prayers to defeat fear comes straight from the Bible.

For God has not given us a spirit of fear, but of power and of love and of a sound mind.
2 TIMOTHY 1:7 NKJV

I pray something like this. *Lord, you did not give me a spirit of fear. No, you didn't. You gave to me a spirit of power and you gave me love and I have a sound mind, therefore, I am not afraid. In Jesus' name. AMEN*

I would speak this prayer aloud often at night when something would startle me awake. It is effective. Repeat it until the fear departs.

Release the power of Jesus through blessings that fill our soul and mind with the Kingdom of light. And when that pesky old devil tries to revisit, we are filled with the love of Christ. And the light within will not allow the devil to return. As the word of God says:

Submit yourselves, then, to God. Resist the devil, and he will flee from you.
JAMES 4:7

THE SIMPLE STEPS

Lynn

Love the Lord your God with all your heart and with all your soul and with all your strength and with all your mind; and, Love your neighbor as yourself.
LUKE 10:27

1. Know you aren't alone. There is hope and answers for you and your family.
2. Believe and affirm your child.
3. Persistently pray in faith that God hears you and will respond.
4. Fear is powerless in the light of love and truth of Jesus.
5. Empower your child with their identity and authority in Christ.
6. Close the open doors and change the atmosphere.
7. Process with Jesus: Teach your child to ask questions and learn from their experience.
8. Coach your child by asking questions to uncover their specific gifts and help discover in what manner they operate (senses).
9. Develop your child's gifting through encouragement and listening to their hints. Make your child's gift a

normal part of life. Ask your child about their encounters and respond with encouragement to share.

10. Protect their gifting and dedicate it to the Kingdom of God.

11. Make the *Power of Blessing* a daily part of your life. Bless your child, your home, your family. Bless, bless, and bless. Release the Kingdom of light into every area of your life. Teach your children to bless. Prayers of blessings change nations!

These simple steps help lead children into a divine connection with God and teach them to respond to his loving voice.

The simple steps outlined in this book are derived from our common experiences within the spiritual realm. The steps don't comprise a defined list of rules and hard-and-fast boundaries. That's because the spiritual realm is a Kingdom. This Kingdom has a King. The King is the creator of all, the Lord, Yahweh. And King Yahweh is good, and he desires a relationship with his children on earth. This is the greatest wonder of the world.

Relationships, however, require time and interest. Relationships are a living construct which grows and changes over time. With this in mind, the simple steps outlined are guidelines to assist you and your family. They point you toward God the Father, who is the giver of all the gifts, and Jesus, whom all authority on earth has been given. Christ shares his authority with God's children and the Holy Spirit that is the power of God.

The simple steps in this book are tremendously helpful. They are powerful when we understand that everything in the spiritual realm is under the authority and love of our good Father. Pray and talk with God often and teach your kids to do the same. Ask him questions. Learn to love and you will experience a life of love and fulfillment.

Shalom, Ann Marie Mora and Lynn Donovan

APPENDIX A

WHAT IS SALVATION?

Ann Marie

My daughter, Carly, walked her father into salvation when she was merely two years old with a simple explanation of where Jesus lives. This moment was extraordinary. I believe her innocent conversation with her dad changed the course of our family and will affect future generations forever. What we didn't understand at the time was that she was gazing directly into the spiritual realm.

HUSBAND'S SALVATION

Ann Marie

In the early years of our marriage, my husband adamantly maintained that God wasn't real. This faith difference became apparent as I longed to teach my children about faith but was uncomfortable because our faith positions created discord in our home.

I remember discussing my faith with Joshua frequently. In fact, I nagged. I was convinced that teaching Godly morals to our kids was right. Finally, questions from my six- and nine-year-old boys began to emerge at the dinner table. Even in their young ages, they recognized that dad didn't believe like mom.

I began attending church with my daughter and spoke often with mentors who encouraged me to refrain from nagging and continue to attend church. They assured me my husband would notice the changes within and become curious. But it was difficult not to apply pressure upon him.

As the months passed, I felt alone and realized I faced a long life with an unbeliever. I knew our faith differences caused confusion for my kids. I wanted to raise my kids to know Jesus. The word divorce arose. In my zeal, I finally issued an ultimatum. Surely, he would comprehend the importance of faith in our lives. This season in my life was difficult. And I do not recommend divorce or issuing an ultimatum, as these challenges strain your marriage further.

Leaning on Jesus, I chose to dig deep and to love my husband with all my heart and to declare the love of God into his heart by praying daily, "Father, I come before you boldly and confidently that you would soften my husband's heart toward you and give him an encounter with you that he cannot deny. I declare in Jesus' name that each member in my home believes in Jesus and finds the Word sweeter than honey from a comb. Amen." Slowly his heart began to soften.

One ordinary evening, I settled the boys into their bedroom to read to them from their newly purchased children's Bible. Carly saw me pick up the boys' Bibles. She proceeded to scoop up her toddler Bible and I watched her place it into her dad's hands. Her innocent eyes looked up, "Daddy, will you read this with me?"

He took her hand and they walked into her bedroom. While he was reading, Carly touched his arm. He looked into her tiny face as she smiled and said, "Daddy, where does Jesus live?" He proceeded to explain, pointing up. "He lives up there, in heaven."

She patted her hand on her bed and replied tenderly and matter-of-factly, "No Daddy, Jesus lives right here."

I tucked the boys in, turned out the light, then stepped into the hallway. My husband stood waiting. He immediately drew me close, holding me against him tighter than ever before. Then simply said, "Carly got me. I'm convinced!"

A two-year-old revealed to my husband that Jesus was real. My heart leapt. Then I cried. And finally, I thanked the Lord in my prayers that evening.

It wasn't the nagging, bitterness, the ultimatum, or anything else that brought my husband to Jesus. It was a little girl who learned to speak only a few months prior. A little girl with a pure heart not yet tainted by the hurts of this world.

In that moment I began to understand that God's intentions for our beautiful baby girl were profound.

APPENDIX B

SIMPLE STEPS TO SALVATION

- Recognize our need for Jesus.
- Accept that God is merciful and loves people, right where they are.
- All the wrong things we've done or things we didn't do but should have, confess your sorrow and repent. All is cleansed by the death, resurrection, and the blood of Jesus.
- Through the Holy Spirit, learn to live a renewed life centered upon biblical principles.
- Understand that our restoration to our Father in heaven arrives to us through his grace and there is nothing we must do to earn it or receive it in return.
- Live and thrive in the hope we have for our earthly lives as well as our eternal life in heaven.

And for the children:

- Explain to your child that Jesus died on a cross and shed his blood to cover our sins. Read the stories about Jesus to your child from a children's Bible.

- Ask your child if they believe the stories about Jesus and prompt them to ask Jesus to come into their heart and to be their friend and helper.
- Pray with your child.

SIMPLE SALVATION PRAYER

A simple prayer:

Jesus, I believe in you. I thank you for washing away every single sin of mine. Please forgive me, today. Jesus, will you and the Holy Spirit come into my heart and live forever and teach me to be your friend and follower. Thank you. In your name, Jesus. Amen

In the same way, I tell you, there is rejoicing in the presence of the angels of God over one sinner who repents.
LUKE 15:10

RESOURCES

Visit AnnMarieMora.com for more topics such as:

- Successful Bedtime Routines
- Healing Stories
- Guiding Others
- Spiritually Cleanse Your Home
- Book Suggestions
- Video Teaching
- Spiritual Gifts Scriptures

READ LYNN'S OTHER BOOKS

Kingdom Conversations
by Lynn Donovan

Marching Around Jericho
by Lynn Donovan

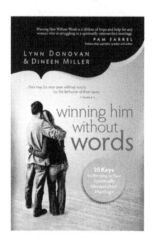

Winning Him Without Words
by Lynn Donovan & Dineen Miller

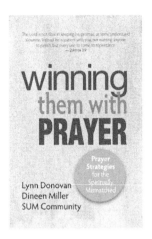

Winning Them with Prayer
by Lynn Donovan & Dineen Miller

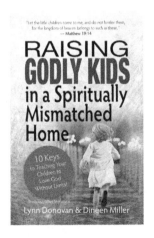

Raising Godly Kids
by Lynn Donovan & Dineen Miller

Made in the USA
Coppell, TX
26 August 2021

61243236R10075